Agentic RAG

Architecting Autonomous AI Systems with Retrieval-Augmented Generation

Camila Jones

Copyright

Table of Content

Preface

Welcome **to "Agentic RAG: Architecting Autonomous AI Systems with Retrieval-Augmented Generation**." This book is a comprehensive guide designed to help researchers, engineers, and AI enthusiasts bridge the gap between theory and practice in the realm of advanced AI systems. By integrating retrieval-augmented generation with autonomous decision-making capabilities, Agentic RAG represents a cutting-edge approach that can power a new generation of intelligent systems.

In this preface, we outline the essential **components that set the stage for the rest of the book:**

- Acknowledgements
- About the Author(s)
- How to Use This Book
- Overview of the Agentic RAG Landscape

Each section is intended to provide you with a strong foundation as you embark on your journey through the material presented in the chapters ahead.

Acknowledgements

This book is the result of a collaborative effort and would not have been possible without the support and contributions of many dedicated individuals. We extend our heartfelt thanks to:

- Research Collaborators: Your innovative ideas and thorough analyses have been crucial in shaping the concepts and methodologies described here.
- Industry Partners: Thank you for sharing real-world challenges and case studies that have enriched the practical components of this book.
- Academic Advisors and Peer Reviewers: Your critical feedback ensured that every technical detail is accurate and that the content remains clear and relevant.
- The Open-Source Community: The tools, libraries, and shared knowledge from this vibrant community have been indispensable in developing the hands-on examples and experiments.
- Family and Friends: Your unwavering support and encouragement have been a source of inspiration throughout this journey.

We are deeply grateful to all who have contributed their time, expertise, and passion to bring this work to fruition.

How to Use This Book

"Agentic RAG" is structured to cater to both the theoretical and practical needs of its readers. Whether you are looking to deepen your understanding of the underlying algorithms or implement hands-on projects, the book is organized to guide you step by step.

Structure of the Book

- Chapters: Each chapter builds on the previous one. Early chapters establish foundational concepts, while later chapters delve into system design, implementation strategies, and case studies.
- Hands-On Examples: Throughout the book, you will encounter detailed code snippets, diagrams, and step-by-step tutorials. These practical examples are designed to be executed as-is or adapted to your specific needs.
- Case Studies: Real-world applications demonstrate how Agentic RAG systems can be deployed across various industries, providing context and inspiration.
- Appendices: Supplementary materials—including a glossary, additional resources, and complete code repositories—are available to help you explore topics in greater depth.

Recommended Prerequisites

To get the most out of this book, we suggest that readers have a basic familiarity with the following areas:

Topic	Recommended Knowledge	Suggested Resources
Machine Learning Basics	Fundamental principles of machine learning	Introductory courses (e.g., Coursera, edX)
Python Programming	Intermediate Python, including libraries like NumPy and Pandas	Official Python documentation, online tutorials
Deep Learning	Basics of neural networks and deep learning architectures	TensorFlow and PyTorch documentation
AI System Design	Understanding of distributed systems and architectural concepts	Research articles and industry whitepapers

Feel free to refer back to this table as you prepare to engage with the content. We recommend having a Python development environment set up (e.g., Jupyter Notebook or a similar IDE) to try out the code examples provided.

Navigating the Book

- For Beginners: Start at the beginning and work through each chapter sequentially. The foundational chapters are designed to build your understanding gradually.
- For Practitioners: You might prefer to focus on the later chapters that cover implementation strategies, case studies, and real-world applications. The detailed code examples and practical tips are immediately applicable.

- For Researchers: The theoretical sections, enriched with recent advances and comparative analyses, offer insights that can inspire new research directions.

Overview of the Agentic RAG Landscape

The landscape of artificial intelligence is rapidly evolving, and two paradigms have emerged as especially transformative: Retrieval-Augmented Generation (RAG) and autonomous decision-making.

What is Retrieval-Augmented Generation (RAG)?

RAG is a hybrid approach that combines the strengths of traditional retrieval methods with modern generative models. Rather than relying solely on a model's internal knowledge, RAG systems access external data sources to enhance the generation process. This results in outputs that are:

- More Accurate: By grounding responses in verifiable data.
- Context-Aware: By integrating relevant information dynamically.
- Adaptable: To various applications, from conversational agents to document summarization.

What Does "Agentic" Mean in This Context?

An agentic system is one that possesses the ability to make autonomous decisions based on its environment and internal models. **When applied to RAG, this means:**

- Autonomous Decision-Making: The system can choose the best course of action (e.g., which information to retrieve or how to generate a response) without human intervention.
- Real-Time Adaptation: The system continuously learns and adapts, optimizing its performance as it processes new data.
- Integrated Feedback Loops: Decisions are refined based on outcomes, creating a self-improving loop that enhances both retrieval and generation processes.

The Significance of Agentic RAG

By merging these two paradigms, Agentic RAG systems offer a unique advantage:

- Enhanced Performance: They deliver more relevant, accurate, and timely information.
- Broad Applicability: From healthcare and finance to robotics and customer service, the potential applications are vast.
- Future-Proofing AI: As data sources expand and environments become more dynamic, the need for systems that can autonomously adapt becomes increasingly critical.

This book delves deep into both the theory and the practical implementation of Agentic RAG systems. You will learn how to architect these systems from the ground up, develop robust data pipelines, integrate cutting-edge retrieval and generation modules, and embed sophisticated decision-making algorithms. Whether you aim to implement these systems in your projects or contribute to future research, this guide provides the tools and insights you need to succeed.

I hope this preface has set a clear and inviting stage for your journey into the world of **Agentic RAG**. As you progress through the chapters, you'll find that every concept is explained step by step, every code example is complete and well annotated, and every case study is chosen to illustrate the real-world impact of these technologies. Welcome aboard, and let's embark on this exploration of autonomous AI systems together.

Chapter 1: Introduction

In this chapter, we set the stage for the journey into Agentic Retrieval-Augmented Generation (RAG) systems. We begin by exploring the evolution of artificial intelligence (AI) and the growing importance of autonomy in modern systems. Next, we define what RAG means in today's AI landscape, explain the concept of an "agentic" system, and outline the scope, audience, and objectives of this book. Finally, we provide a roadmap that guides you through the content in the chapters that follow.

1.1 The Evolution of AI and the Rise of Autonomy

Historical Context and Motivations

The field of AI has evolved dramatically over the past several decades. Early AI research focused on symbolic logic and rule-based systems. Over time, the development of statistical methods and machine learning algorithms paved the way for the deep learning revolution that now underpins many modern AI applications.

Timeline of Key Milestones in AI:

Year	Milestone	Significance
1950s	Turing Test, Early Rule-Based Systems	Laid the conceptual groundwork for machine intelligence
1960s-70s	Development of Expert Systems	Introduced practical applications of AI in limited domains
1980s	Rise of Neural Networks	Provided a new paradigm for pattern recognition and learning
1990s	Statistical Machine Learning	Enhanced data-driven approaches and probabilistic reasoning
2000s	Deep Learning Revolution	Enabled breakthroughs in computer vision, speech recognition, etc.
2010s	Transformer Models and Large-Scale Pretrained Models	Revolutionized natural language processing (NLP) and generative tasks

2020s	Emergence of Hybrid Models (e.g., RAG) and Autonomy in AI	Integration of retrieval techniques and autonomous decision-making

The motivation behind these developments is clear: as the complexity of data and real-world applications increased, so did the need for AI systems that could learn from vast amounts of information, adapt in real time, and operate autonomously. This drive for improved accuracy, efficiency, and adaptability is at the heart of today's AI research and applications.

1.2 Defining Retrieval-Augmented Generation (RAG)

From Pure Generation to Hybrid Models
Traditional generative models, such as those based on sequence-to-sequence architectures, rely solely on internal representations learned during training. While powerful, these models may lack access to up-to-date or specialized external information, which can lead to responses that are generic or even outdated. Retrieval-Augmented Generation (RAG) represents a hybrid approach where the generative process is supplemented by a retrieval mechanism. This dual strategy allows a system to fetch relevant, context-specific data from an external source (e.g., databases, knowledge bases, or document corpora) and incorporate that information into its generated output. This results in outputs that are not only coherent and context-aware but also grounded in real-world data.

A Simple Code Example
Below is a simplified pseudocode example that outlines the basic workflow of a RAG system:
python
Copy code

```python
# Pseudocode for a basic Retrieval-Augmented Generation process

def retrieve_information(query, database):
    """
    Retrieve relevant documents from the database based on the query.
    """
    # Simulate retrieval using keyword matching or vector similarity
    relevant_docs = []
    for doc in database:
        if query in doc['text']:
            relevant_docs.append(doc)
    return relevant_docs
```

```python
def generate_response(query, retrieved_docs, generative_model):
    """
    Generate a response using both the query and the retrieved documents.
    """
    # Combine the query and the context from retrieved documents
    context = " ".join([doc['text'] for doc in retrieved_docs])
    input_text = query + " " + context
    # Generate the response using the generative model (e.g., a transformer)
    response = generative_model.generate(input_text)
    return response

# Example usage:
database = [
    {"id": 1, "text": "Artificial Intelligence has evolved through several phases."},
    {"id": 2, "text": "Deep learning techniques have revolutionized AI in recent years."}
]

query = "What are the major milestones in AI?"
retrieved_docs = retrieve_information(query, database)
response = generate_response(query, retrieved_docs, generative_model)
print("Response:", response)
```

Explanation:
- retrieve_information: This function simulates a retrieval process by scanning a simple database for documents containing the query.
- generate_response: This function merges the original query with the context provided by the retrieved documents and passes the combined text to a generative model.
- The pseudocode demonstrates how RAG leverages both retrieval and generation to produce more informed outputs.

1.3 What Makes a System "Agentic"?

Integrating Autonomous Decision-Making

The term "agentic" in the context of AI refers to a system's ability to act independently by making decisions based on its environment and internal models. An agentic system is not merely reactive; it actively assesses situations and chooses actions to achieve its objectives.

For example, consider an AI-powered customer support bot:

- Traditional Model: It may simply generate responses based on pre-learned patterns.
- Agentic Model: It evaluates the conversation context, retrieves relevant information, and autonomously decides which response strategy will most effectively address the customer's issue.

Key Elements of an Agentic System

1. Autonomy: The ability to operate without human intervention by making independent decisions.
2. Adaptability: The capacity to learn from new data and adjust actions in real time.
3. Feedback Integration: Continuous improvement through monitoring outcomes and refining decision-making policies.

Simple Decision-Making Example

Below is a simplified pseudocode snippet that illustrates how a decision engine might select an action based on a set of retrieved information:

python

Copy code

```python
def decision_engine(retrieved_docs):
    """
    Decide on the best action based on the content of retrieved documents.
    """
    # Simple decision logic: prioritize documents based on relevance score
    sorted_docs = sorted(retrieved_docs, key=lambda doc: doc.get('relevance', 0), reverse=True)
    if sorted_docs and sorted_docs[0]['relevance'] > 0.8:
        return "generate_detailed_response"
    else:
        return "ask_for_clarification"

# Example usage:
action = decision_engine(retrieved_docs)
print("Chosen action:", action)
```

Explanation:

- The decision_engine function sorts retrieved documents based on a hypothetical "relevance" score.
- Depending on the top document's relevance, the system either proceeds to generate a detailed response or opts to ask for clarification.

- This example highlights the integration of autonomous decision-making within a RAG framework.

1.4 Scope, Audience, and Objectives of the Book

Scope

This book is a comprehensive resource that covers:
- The theoretical foundations of both retrieval-augmented generation and autonomous decision-making.
- Practical implementation techniques, including data preprocessing, module integration, and system optimization.
- Real-world case studies demonstrating the application of Agentic RAG systems across various industries.
- Ethical, legal, and societal considerations associated with deploying autonomous AI systems.

Intended Audience

This book is written for:
- Researchers: Interested in the latest academic advances and future research directions in AI.
- Engineers: Seeking hands-on guidance to implement and deploy advanced AI systems.
- Industry Professionals: Looking for practical case studies and strategies to integrate AI into real-world applications.
- Advanced Students: Eager to learn about state-of-the-art AI architectures and contribute to innovative projects.

Objectives

By the end of this book, readers will:
- Understand the evolution and significance of AI and autonomous systems.
- Gain a deep understanding of Retrieval-Augmented Generation (RAG) and its practical benefits.
- Learn how to design, implement, and optimize Agentic RAG systems.
- Be equipped with the skills to apply these technologies in diverse domains.
- Develop a critical understanding of the ethical and societal implications of autonomous AI.

1.5 Structure and Roadmap

The book is organized into clearly defined chapters that gradually build your knowledge and skills:

- Chapters 1-4: Introduce foundational concepts—ranging from the evolution of AI to the principles of autonomous decision-making and the basics of RAG.
- Chapters 5-10: Focus on system architecture, data pipelines, and detailed module development. These chapters include hands-on code examples, design patterns, and optimization strategies.
- Chapters 11-13: Provide practical implementation strategies, case studies, and experimental designs to help you build and benchmark Agentic RAG systems.
- Chapters 14-16: Explore the ethical, legal, and societal aspects of autonomous AI, future trends, and final reflections.

Roadmap Table:

Chapter	Focus Area	Key Topics Covered
1	Introduction	Evolution of AI, RAG definition, agentic systems, scope & roadmap
2-4	Theoretical Foundations	Machine learning, decision theory, neural architectures, retrieval methods
5-10	System Design & Implementation	Architecture, data pipelines, module integration, optimization
11-13	Practical Applications	Coding tutorials, case studies, experimental design, benchmarking
14-16	Future Perspectives & Ethical Considerations	Ethics, legal aspects, emerging trends, final thoughts

This structured roadmap is designed to help you navigate the content effectively, whether you're reading sequentially for a deep dive or referring to specific sections as needed.

In summary, this introductory chapter lays the groundwork for understanding both the evolution of AI and the innovative fusion of retrieval-augmented generation with autonomous decision-making. As you progress through the book, each chapter will build upon these foundational ideas with hands-on examples, clear explanations, and practical insights—all designed to empower you to create next-generation AI systems.

Chapter 2: Theoretical Foundations in AI and Autonomous Systems

In this chapter, we lay the theoretical groundwork for understanding modern AI systems. We begin with the essential concepts of machine learning and deep learning, move into decision theory and reinforcement learning, explore the evolution of neural architectures from RNNs to Transformers, and conclude with an overview of retrieval techniques and algorithms.

2.1 Core Concepts in Machine Learning and Deep Learning

What Is Machine Learning?

Machine Learning (ML) is a subfield of artificial intelligence that focuses on enabling computers to learn patterns from data without being explicitly programmed. It is broadly divided into:

- Supervised Learning: The model learns from labeled data (e.g., classification, regression).
- Unsupervised Learning: The model identifies patterns or clusters in unlabeled data (e.g., clustering, dimensionality reduction).
- Semi-Supervised Learning: Combines a small amount of labeled data with a large amount of unlabeled data.
- Reinforcement Learning: The model learns by interacting with an environment, receiving rewards or penalties.

What Is Deep Learning?

Deep Learning (DL) is a subset of machine learning that uses neural networks with multiple layers (hence "deep") to model complex patterns in large datasets. Deep learning has driven significant breakthroughs in computer vision, natural language processing, and speech recognition.

Key Concepts and Terminology

Term	Description
Neuron	Basic unit in a neural network that computes a weighted sum of its inputs and applies an activation function.
Layer	A collection of neurons; layers are stacked to form a neural network.

Activation Function	A non-linear function (e.g., ReLU, sigmoid) applied to the neuron's output to introduce non-linearity.
Loss Function	Measures the difference between the predicted output and the actual output (e.g., mean squared error, cross-entropy).
Optimizer	Algorithm used to minimize the loss function (e.g., SGD, Adam).

A Simple Deep Learning Example

Below is a complete and well-commented Python code example using PyTorch. This example demonstrates a basic neural network for classifying the MNIST dataset.

python

Copy code

```python
# Import necessary libraries
import torch
import torch.nn as nn
import torch.optim as optim
from torchvision import datasets, transforms
from torch.utils.data import DataLoader

# Define a simple neural network architecture
class SimpleNN(nn.Module):
    def __init__(self):
        super(SimpleNN, self).__init__()
        # Define a network with one hidden layer
        self.fc1 = nn.Linear(28 * 28, 128)  # Input layer to hidden layer
        self.relu = nn.ReLU()           # Activation function
        self.fc2 = nn.Linear(128, 10)     # Hidden layer to output layer

    def forward(self, x):
        # Flatten the image into a vector
        x = x.view(-1, 28 * 28)
        x = self.fc1(x)
        x = self.relu(x)
        x = self.fc2(x)
        return x

# Set up data transformations and load the MNIST dataset
```

```python
transform = transforms.Compose([transforms.ToTensor()])
train_dataset = datasets.MNIST(root='./data', train=True,
transform=transform, download=True)
train_loader = DataLoader(dataset=train_dataset, batch_size=64,
shuffle=True)

# Initialize the neural network, loss function, and optimizer
model = SimpleNN()
criterion = nn.CrossEntropyLoss()
optimizer = optim.Adam(model.parameters(), lr=0.001)

# Training loop for one epoch
for epoch in range(1):
    for batch_idx, (data, target) in enumerate(train_loader):
        optimizer.zero_grad()       # Clear gradients from the previous step
        output = model(data)        # Forward pass
        loss = criterion(output, target)  # Compute loss
        loss.backward()             # Backpropagation to compute gradients
        optimizer.step()            # Update model parameters

        if batch_idx % 100 == 0:
            print(f'Batch {batch_idx}: Loss = {loss.item():.4f}')

print("Training complete!")
```

Explanation:
- Data Loading: The MNIST dataset is loaded and transformed into tensors.
- Model Definition: A simple fully connected neural network is defined with one hidden layer and a ReLU activation function.
- Training Loop: The model is trained for one epoch. At each step, the loss is computed and backpropagated, and the optimizer updates the model weights.

2.2 An Introduction to Decision Theory and Reinforcement Learning

Decision Theory Overview
Decision Theory deals with the principles and models used to make rational decisions under uncertainty. It provides a mathematical framework to analyze choices by evaluating outcomes based on probabilities and utilities.
- Utility: A measure of the satisfaction or benefit derived from an outcome.

- Risk: The potential variability in outcomes.
- Expected Value: The weighted average of all possible outcomes, where each outcome is weighted by its probability.

Reinforcement Learning (RL)

Reinforcement Learning is an area of machine learning where an agent learns to make decisions by interacting with an environment. The agent receives rewards or penalties based on its actions, with the goal of maximizing cumulative reward.

Key Components of RL:

Component	Description
Agent	The decision-maker.
Environment	The external system with which the agent interacts.
State	A representation of the current situation of the environment.
Action	Choices available to the agent.
Reward	Feedback signal indicating the success of an action.
Policy	A strategy used by the agent to decide its actions based on the current state.

Simple Q-Learning Example

Below is a simplified Python pseudocode example of a Q-learning algorithm for a grid-world environment:

python
Copy code

```python
import numpy as np

# Initialize parameters
num_states = 16      # For a 4x4 grid
num_actions = 4      # Up, Down, Left, Right
Q = np.zeros((num_states, num_actions)) # Q-table initialization

alpha = 0.1          # Learning rate
gamma = 0.9          # Discount factor
epsilon = 0.2        # Exploration probability
num_episodes = 1000  # Number of episodes
```

```python
def choose_action(state):
    if np.random.uniform(0, 1) < epsilon:
        # Explore: choose a random action
        return np.random.choice(num_actions)
    else:
        # Exploit: choose the best known action
        return np.argmax(Q[state, :])

def get_next_state(state, action):
    # Define state transition logic for a 4x4 grid (simplified)
    # This function should return the next state given current state and
    action.
    # For brevity, we assume a deterministic function.
    return (state + action) % num_states

def get_reward(state, action, next_state):
    # Define a reward function. For example:
    # +1 for reaching a goal state (say state 15), 0 otherwise.
    return 1 if next_state == 15 else 0

# Q-Learning algorithm
for episode in range(num_episodes):
    state = np.random.randint(0, num_states)  # Start from a random state
    done = False
    while not done:
        action = choose_action(state)
        next_state = get_next_state(state, action)
        reward = get_reward(state, action, next_state)

        # Update Q-Value using the Bellman Equation
        Q[state, action] = Q[state, action] + alpha * (
            reward + gamma * np.max(Q[next_state, :]) - Q[state, action])

        state = next_state

        # Assume the episode ends if the agent reaches state 15
        if state == 15:
            done = True

print("Q-Learning complete. Final Q-Table:")
print(Q)
```

Explanation:

- Q-Table: Stores the estimated rewards for state-action pairs.
- Exploration vs. Exploitation: Controlled by epsilon, which determines whether the agent explores or exploits.
- State Transitions and Rewards: Functions simulate environment dynamics.
- Bellman Equation: Used to update Q-values iteratively.

2.3 Neural Architectures: From RNNs to Transformers

Recurrent Neural Networks (RNNs)

RNNs are designed for sequential data. They maintain an internal state that captures information about previous inputs, making them useful for tasks like time series analysis and language modeling. However, they often struggle with long-term dependencies due to issues like vanishing gradients.

Simple RNN Example (Pseudocode):

python

Copy code

```python
import torch
import torch.nn as nn

class SimpleRNN(nn.Module):
    def __init__(self, input_size, hidden_size, output_size):
        super(SimpleRNN, self).__init__()
        self.hidden_size = hidden_size
        self.rnn = nn.RNN(input_size, hidden_size, batch_first=True)
        self.fc = nn.Linear(hidden_size, output_size)

    def forward(self, x):
        # x: [batch_size, sequence_length, input_size]
        out, hidden = self.rnn(x)  # out: [batch_size, sequence_length, hidden_size]
        # Taking the output from the last time step
        out = self.fc(out[:, -1, :])
        return out

# Example usage:
input_size = 10
hidden_size = 20
output_size = 2
```

```python
model_rnn = SimpleRNN(input_size, hidden_size, output_size)
print(model_rnn)
```

Explanation:
- RNN Layer: Processes sequential data.
- Fully Connected Layer: Maps the hidden state at the final time step to the output.
- This simple example demonstrates an RNN that can be extended for tasks such as language modeling or time-series prediction.

Transformers

Transformers have revolutionized natural language processing by using self-attention mechanisms to model dependencies without relying on sequential processing. This allows them to capture long-range dependencies more efficiently.

Key Differences between RNNs and Transformers:

Aspect	RNNs	Transformers
Sequence Processing	Processes data sequentially	Processes data in parallel via self-attention
Handling Long-Term Dependencies	May struggle due to vanishing gradients	Handles long-range dependencies effectively
Training Efficiency	Generally slower due to sequential nature	Highly parallelizable, faster on large datasets

Basic Transformer Block (Conceptual Pseudocode):

python

Copy code

```python
import torch
import torch.nn as nn

class SimpleTransformerBlock(nn.Module):
    def __init__(self, embed_size, heads):
        super(SimpleTransformerBlock, self).__init__()
        self.attention = nn.MultiheadAttention(embed_dim=embed_size,
num_heads=heads, batch_first=True)
        self.feed_forward = nn.Sequential(
            nn.Linear(embed_size, embed_size * 4),
            nn.ReLU(),
            nn.Linear(embed_size * 4, embed_size)
        )
        self.layer_norm1 = nn.LayerNorm(embed_size)
```

```
    self.layer_norm2 = nn.LayerNorm(embed_size)

  def forward(self, x):
    # Self-attention layer with residual connection
    attn_output, _ = self.attention(x, x, x)
    x = self.layer_norm1(x + attn_output)
    # Feed-forward network with residual connection
    ff_output = self.feed_forward(x)
    x = self.layer_norm2(x + ff_output)
    return x

# Example usage:
embed_size = 64
heads = 8
transformer_block = SimpleTransformerBlock(embed_size, heads)
sample_input = torch.rand(32, 10, embed_size)  # [batch_size,
sequence_length, embed_size]
output = transformer_block(sample_input)
print("Transformer Block Output Shape:", output.shape)
```

Explanation:
- Multi-Head Attention: Allows the model to focus on different parts of the sequence simultaneously.
- Feed-Forward Network: Provides non-linear transformations.
- Layer Normalization and Residual Connections: Ensure training stability and effective gradient flow.

2.4 Overview of Retrieval Techniques and Algorithms

Traditional Retrieval Methods
Traditional information retrieval relies on methods such as:
- Keyword Matching: Simple text matching to retrieve documents containing query terms.
- TF-IDF (Term Frequency-Inverse Document Frequency): Weighs words by importance relative to a document corpus.
- BM25: A ranking function used by many search engines that considers term frequency, document length, and other factors.

Neural Retrieval Methods

Recent advances have introduced neural retrieval methods that leverage deep learning to produce dense vector representations (embeddings) for both queries and documents. This allows retrieval based on semantic similarity rather than simple keyword overlap.

Cosine Similarity Example:

Below is a Python example that computes cosine similarity between a query embedding and document embeddings using the numpy library:

python

Copy code

```python
import numpy as np

def cosine_similarity(vec1, vec2):
    """Calculate the cosine similarity between two vectors."""
    dot_product = np.dot(vec1, vec2)
    norm_vec1 = np.linalg.norm(vec1)
    norm_vec2 = np.linalg.norm(vec2)
    return dot_product / (norm_vec1 * norm_vec2)

# Example embeddings (for demonstration purposes)
query_embedding = np.array([0.5, 0.1, 0.3])
doc_embedding_1 = np.array([0.4, 0.2, 0.4])
doc_embedding_2 = np.array([0.1, 0.3, 0.2])

similarity_1 = cosine_similarity(query_embedding, doc_embedding_1)
similarity_2 = cosine_similarity(query_embedding, doc_embedding_2)

print("Cosine Similarity with Document 1:", similarity_1)
print("Cosine Similarity with Document 2:", similarity_2)
```

Explanation:
- Cosine Similarity Function: Computes the similarity score between two vectors.
- Usage: In a retrieval system, the query embedding is compared with document embeddings to rank the documents by relevance.

Hybrid Retrieval Techniques

Modern systems often combine traditional and neural methods to achieve both precision and recall. For example:
- Initial Candidate Generation: Use keyword matching or BM25 to narrow down the document set.
- Re-Ranking: Use neural embeddings and cosine similarity to re-rank the candidates based on semantic relevance.

Summary

In this chapter, we provided a thorough grounding in the theoretical foundations that underpin modern AI and autonomous systems:

- Machine Learning and Deep Learning: We covered basic principles, key terminology, and provided a simple neural network example.
- Decision Theory and Reinforcement Learning: We introduced fundamental concepts and illustrated Q-learning with pseudocode.
- Neural Architectures: We traced the evolution from RNNs to Transformers, highlighting their respective advantages.
- Retrieval Techniques: We compared traditional methods with modern neural approaches, including a practical cosine similarity example.

This foundational knowledge sets the stage for the practical and advanced topics discussed in later chapters, enabling you to build and understand Agentic RAG systems from both a theoretical and hands-on perspective.

Chapter 3: Fundamentals of Retrieval-Augmented Generation (RAG)

Retrieval-Augmented Generation (RAG) is an innovative approach that combines traditional retrieval methods with modern generative models. This fusion allows AI systems to generate responses that are both contextually relevant and enriched by external, verifiable information. In this chapter, we explore the principles behind RAG, break down its key components, compare it with conventional AI approaches, and review recent state-of-the-art advances in the field.

3.1 The RAG Paradigm: Principles and Evolution

Principles of RAG

At its core, the RAG paradigm is built on the idea that generative models, such as large language models (LLMs), can be significantly enhanced by incorporating an external retrieval mechanism. Rather than relying solely on the internal parameters learned during training, a RAG system augments its responses by fetching relevant information from an external knowledge base or document corpus. This approach provides several benefits:

- Improved Accuracy: Responses are grounded in external data, reducing the risk of generating outdated or incorrect information.
- Enhanced Contextualization: By retrieving contextually relevant data, the generated output can better address complex queries.
- Adaptability: The system can adapt to new information without requiring a complete retraining of the generative model.

Evolution of the RAG Paradigm

The evolution of RAG reflects the broader shifts in AI research—from purely generative approaches to hybrid models that leverage both retrieval and generation. Key milestones in this evolution include:

- Early Generative Models: Initially, models such as sequence-to-sequence networks and early LLMs generated responses solely based on internal training data.
- Introduction of Retrieval Methods: Techniques such as TF-IDF and BM25 were incorporated into early systems to bring in relevant external information.
- Neural Retrieval Models: With the advent of deep learning, dense vector representations and neural retrieval models emerged, enabling semantic matching rather than simple keyword overlap.
- Hybrid Architectures: Recent years have seen the formalization of the RAG approach, where dedicated retrieval modules are integrated seamlessly with powerful generative models (e.g., using transformer architectures).

These developments have transformed the way AI systems handle knowledge, leading to more accurate and context-aware applications.

3.2 Key Components: Retrieval Module vs. Generative Module

A RAG system typically consists of two main components that work in tandem:

1. Retrieval Module

The retrieval module is responsible for fetching relevant documents or information from an external source based on the input query. Its key functions include:

- Document Indexing: Organizing the external knowledge base so that it can be searched efficiently.
- Relevance Scoring: Using algorithms (such as cosine similarity or BM25) to rank documents based on their relevance to the query.
- Candidate Generation: Producing a shortlist of documents or data snippets that will be used to inform the generative process.

2. Generative Module

The generative module takes the input query along with the context provided by the retrieved documents and produces the final output. Its responsibilities include:

- Context Integration: Combining the original query with the retrieved information.
- Response Generation: Using a language model (e.g., a transformer-based model) to generate coherent and contextually enriched responses.
- Output Refinement: Optionally, applying post-processing to ensure that the response adheres to desired quality and relevance standards.

Comparative Table

Below is a table that highlights the differences between the retrieval and generative modules:

Aspect	Retrieval Module	Generative Module
Primary Function	Fetch relevant external data	Generate responses using learned language patterns
Techniques Used	Keyword matching, TF-IDF, BM25, dense vector embeddings	Transformer models, sequence-to-sequence architectures
Data Source	External databases,	Pre-trained internal parameters from large

	knowledge bases, document corpora	datasets
Output	Ranked list of documents or text snippets	Coherent text response, integrating retrieved context

A Simple RAG Code Example

Below is a simplified Python pseudocode example that demonstrates how a RAG system might operate by combining a retrieval module with a generative module:

python

Copy code

```python
import numpy as np

# --- Retrieval Module ---
def simple_retrieval(query, corpus):
    """
    Retrieve documents from the corpus that contain keywords from the query.
    For simplicity, we use keyword matching.
    """
    retrieved_docs = []
    for doc in corpus:
        if any(word.lower() in doc.lower() for word in query.split()):
            retrieved_docs.append(doc)
    return retrieved_docs

# --- Generative Module ---
def simple_generation(query, retrieved_docs):
    """
    Generate a response by combining the query with the retrieved documents.
    A real implementation would use a transformer model; here we simulate with string concatenation.
    """
    context = " ".join(retrieved_docs)
    response = f"Query: {query}\nContext: {context}\nGenerated Answer: [Simulated response based on combined information]"
    return response

# Example usage:
```

```
corpus = [
    "Artificial Intelligence has evolved significantly over the last few
decades.",
    "Hybrid models that integrate retrieval and generation have shown
improved accuracy.",
    "Recent advances in transformer models have revolutionized language
understanding."
]

query = "How has AI evolved with hybrid models?"
retrieved_docs = simple_retrieval(query, corpus)
response = simple_generation(query, retrieved_docs)
print("Response:\n", response)
```

Explanation:
- simple_retrieval: This function mimics a retrieval process by checking if words from the query exist in the document text.
- simple_generation: This function simulates generation by concatenating the query with the retrieved context. In a production system, a transformer model would generate a nuanced response based on the input.
- The example illustrates the core idea of RAG: using external information to enhance the generated answer.

3.3 Comparative Analysis with Traditional AI Models

Traditional Generative Models

Traditional generative models, such as those solely based on neural language models, generate responses using only the data encoded during training. While these models can produce fluent text, they may lack the ability to:
- Incorporate Real-Time Information: They rely on static training data and may not reflect recent developments or specific domain knowledge.
- Ground Responses in External Sources: Without retrieval, responses might be generic or factually imprecise.

Advantages of RAG over Traditional Models

Feature	Traditional Generative Models	RAG Systems
Information Source	Internal, static training data	Combination of internal data and external, dynamic sources

Context Awareness	Limited to learned representations	Enhanced by retrieving up-to-date and context-specific data
Adaptability	Requires retraining to update knowledge	Can integrate new information on-the-fly through retrieval
Accuracy	Prone to generating outdated or incorrect information	More reliable due to grounding in verifiable external data

Example Scenario Comparison

Imagine a system tasked with answering questions about recent technological advances. A traditional generative model might rely on outdated training data, resulting in vague or incorrect responses. In contrast, a RAG system can retrieve current articles or papers about recent innovations and generate an informed answer that reflects the latest developments.

3.4 Recent Advances and State-of-the-Art Innovations

The field of RAG is rapidly evolving, with several innovations pushing the boundaries of what hybrid models can achieve. Some notable advances include:

Neural Dense Retrieval

- Dense Vector Embeddings: Models such as Sentence-BERT create high-dimensional embeddings that capture semantic meaning, enabling more accurate retrieval based on conceptual similarity rather than just keyword overlap.
- Dual Encoders: Architectures that encode queries and documents separately, then use cosine similarity for ranking. These models have been shown to outperform traditional sparse retrieval methods in many scenarios.

Improved Generative Models

- Transformer-Based Generators: Large-scale transformers (e.g., GPT-3, T5) are being fine-tuned in RAG systems to generate contextually rich and coherent responses.
- Fusion-in-Decoder (FiD): An advanced method where retrieved documents are integrated within the decoder's attention mechanism, allowing the generative model to consider multiple contexts simultaneously.

End-to-End Training Approaches

- Joint Optimization: Recent research focuses on end-to-end training where both the retrieval and generative modules are optimized together, leading to improved synergy between the components.
- Feedback Loops: Incorporating reinforcement learning techniques to continuously refine the retrieval process based on the quality of the generated output.

Table of Recent Innovations

Innovation	Description	Impact
Dense Retrieval Models	Use of semantic embeddings to retrieve contextually relevant documents	Improved recall and precision in information retrieval
Fusion-in-Decoder (FiD)	Integrates multiple retrieved documents within the generation process	Enhanced contextual understanding and response quality
Joint End-to-End Training	Simultaneous optimization of both retrieval and generation modules	Better alignment between retrieved context and generated output
Reinforcement Learning	Feedback-driven optimization to refine retrieval strategies	Adaptive systems that improve over time

Code Example for a Dense Retrieval Scenario

Below is a simplified example using Python and pseudo-code to demonstrate how dense retrieval might be implemented with vector embeddings:

python

Copy code

```
import numpy as np
from sklearn.metrics.pairwise import cosine_similarity

# Example: Precomputed embeddings for a small corpus
corpus_embeddings = np.array([
    [0.2, 0.1, 0.7],
    [0.6, 0.8, 0.1],
    [0.4, 0.3, 0.9]
])
corpus_documents = [
    "AI has seen tremendous growth in recent years.",
```

```
    "Hybrid models combine retrieval with generation for better
performance.",
    "Dense embeddings capture semantic meaning in text."
]

# Example query embedding (normally obtained from a trained encoder
model)
query_embedding = np.array([[0.3, 0.2, 0.8]])

# Compute cosine similarities between the query and corpus embeddings
similarities = cosine_similarity(query_embedding, corpus_embeddings)
print("Cosine Similarities:", similarities)

# Retrieve the document with the highest similarity
top_index = np.argmax(similarities)
retrieved_doc = corpus_documents[top_index]
print("Retrieved Document:", retrieved_doc)
```

Explanation:
- Embedding Comparison: The code computes cosine similarities between a query embedding and a set of document embeddings.
- Retrieval: The document with the highest similarity score is retrieved. In practice, the embeddings would be generated by a deep learning model (e.g., Sentence-BERT), and the retrieval process would handle large-scale corpora.
- Integration: This dense retrieval process can be integrated into a RAG system where the retrieved document informs the generative model to produce an enhanced response.

Summary
In this chapter, we have explored the fundamentals of Retrieval-Augmented Generation (RAG):
- 3.1 The RAG Paradigm: We reviewed the core principles behind RAG, including its evolution from traditional generative models to hybrid architectures that incorporate external knowledge.
- 3.2 Key Components: We detailed the roles of the retrieval and generative modules, providing a clear comparison and a basic code example.
- 3.3 Comparative Analysis: We contrasted RAG with traditional AI models, highlighting the advantages of using external data to improve context and accuracy.

- 3.4 Recent Advances: We discussed state-of-the-art innovations in dense retrieval, transformer-based generators, and joint training approaches, complete with illustrative tables and code snippets.

This comprehensive understanding of RAG sets the stage for deeper dives into system design and practical implementations in later chapters. Each section is designed to be accessible to technical readers while providing hands-on insights and clear examples to foster a solid grasp of the concepts.

Chapter 4: Autonomous Decision-Making in AI

Autonomous decision-making is a cornerstone of advanced AI systems. In this chapter, we explore what it means for a system to be "autonomous," review various decision-making frameworks, delve into reinforcement learning and policy optimization, and finally, discuss multi-agent systems and distributed decision-making. By the end of this chapter, you will understand both the theoretical underpinnings and practical implementations of autonomous decision-making in AI.

4.1 Defining Autonomy: Concepts and Terminology

Autonomy in AI refers to the capability of a system to operate independently, making decisions based on its environment and internal models without constant human intervention. This quality is essential for applications where real-time, adaptive responses are required, such as robotics, self-driving cars, and intelligent agents in complex systems.

Key Concepts and Terminology

Below is a table summarizing some of the essential terms related to autonomy:

Term	Definition
Autonomous Agent	An entity capable of independent decision-making and actions based on its perceptions.
Policy	A strategy or rule set that the agent follows to decide on actions in a given state.
State	A representation of the current environment or situation in which the agent operates.
Action	A choice or operation the agent can perform in response to its current state.
Reward	A numerical value indicating the benefit of an action, used to guide learning a nd decision-making.
Feedback Loop	A system mechanism that uses the outcomes of decisions to improve future performance.

Autonomy involves not just the ability to act, but also to learn from experience, adapt to changes, and optimize decisions over time. This is often achieved through a combination of predefined rules, learned behaviors, and hybrid approaches that blend both methodologies.

4.2 Decision-Making Frameworks: Rule-Based, Learning-Based, and Hybrid

Decision-making in AI can be broadly classified into three frameworks:

1. Rule-Based Systems

Rule-Based Systems rely on explicitly defined rules that map conditions to actions. They are deterministic and straightforward to design but lack adaptability.

- Advantages:
  - Simple to implement and understand.
  - Predictable and explainable behavior.
- Disadvantages:
  - Poor scalability.
  - Limited flexibility in dynamic environments.

2. Learning-Based Systems

Learning-Based Systems leverage data and experience to learn decision policies. Techniques such as supervised learning, unsupervised learning, and reinforcement learning fall under this category.

- Advantages:
  - Ability to adapt to complex, changing environments.
  - Can improve performance over time.
- Disadvantages:
  - Require large amounts of data.
  - Often behave as "black boxes," making their decisions less transparent.

3. Hybrid Systems

Hybrid Systems combine rule-based methods with learning-based approaches. These systems use predefined rules as a baseline while allowing learning algorithms to adapt or override rules when necessary.

- Advantages:
  - Balance between predictability and adaptability.
  - Can incorporate domain expertise while remaining flexible.
- Disadvantages:
  - More complex to design and integrate.
  - May require careful tuning to avoid conflicts between rules and learned behaviors.

Comparative Table

Framework	Methodology	Strengths	Weaknesses

Rule-Based	Predefined if-then rules	Simple, explainable, predictable	Not adaptive, hard to scale
Learning-Based	Data-driven model learning	Adaptable, scalable, can improve over time	Requires extensive data, less transparent
Hybrid	Combination of rules and learning algorithms	Balances reliability with adaptability	Complexity in integration and tuning

4.3 Reinforcement Learning and Policy Optimization

Reinforcement Learning (RL) is a powerful framework for autonomous decision-making. In RL, an agent interacts with an environment, learns from the rewards or penalties received for its actions, and iteratively improves its policy to maximize cumulative rewards.

Core Concepts in Reinforcement Learning
- Agent: The decision-maker that interacts with the environment.
- Environment: The external system or context with which the agent interacts.
- State: A snapshot of the environment at a given time.
- Action: A decision taken by the agent.
- Reward: Feedback provided by the environment after an action.
- Policy: The strategy used by the agent to decide which action to take.
- Value Function: A measure of the long-term reward expected from a state or state-action pair.

Policy Optimization
Policy optimization involves refining the policy so that the agent's decisions lead to maximum cumulative reward. Two common approaches are:
- Value-Based Methods: Such as Q-learning, where the agent learns a value function that estimates the reward for taking specific actions in given states.
- Policy-Based Methods: Such as REINFORCE, where the agent directly learns a policy that maps states to actions without explicitly learning a value function.

Example: A Simple Policy Gradient (REINFORCE) Implementation
Below is a complete Python example using PyTorch that demonstrates a simplified version of the REINFORCE algorithm. This example uses a common environment (CartPole) from OpenAI Gym:

python
Copy code

```python
import torch
import torch.nn as nn
import torch.optim as optim
import gym
import numpy as np

# Define the Policy Network
class PolicyNetwork(nn.Module):
    def __init__(self, input_dim, hidden_dim, output_dim):
        super(PolicyNetwork, self).__init__()
        self.fc1 = nn.Linear(input_dim, hidden_dim)
        self.relu = nn.ReLU()
        self.fc2 = nn.Linear(hidden_dim, output_dim)
        self.softmax = nn.Softmax(dim=1)

    def forward(self, x):
        x = self.relu(self.fc1(x))
        x = self.fc2(x)
        return self.softmax(x)

# Initialize environment and policy network
env = gym.make('CartPole-v1')
input_dim = env.observation_space.shape[0]
hidden_dim = 128
output_dim = env.action_space.n
policy_net = PolicyNetwork(input_dim, hidden_dim, output_dim)
optimizer = optim.Adam(policy_net.parameters(), lr=1e-2)

# Function to select an action based on policy probabilities
def select_action(state):
    state = torch.from_numpy(state).float().unsqueeze(0)
    probabilities = policy_net(state)
    action = np.random.choice(output_dim,
p=probabilities.detach().numpy()[0])
    log_prob = torch.log(probabilities.squeeze(0)[action])
    return action, log_prob

# Training loop using the REINFORCE algorithm
def train_policy(episodes=500):
    gamma = 0.99  # Discount factor
```

```python
    for episode in range(episodes):
        state = env.reset()
        log_probs = []
        rewards = []
        done = False

        while not done:
            action, log_prob = select_action(state)
            next_state, reward, done, _ = env.step(action)
            log_probs.append(log_prob)
            rewards.append(reward)
            state = next_state

        # Compute discounted rewards
        discounted_rewards = []
        cumulative_reward = 0
        for reward in rewards[::-1]:
            cumulative_reward = reward + gamma * cumulative_reward
            discounted_rewards.insert(0, cumulative_reward)

        # Normalize rewards for stability
        discounted_rewards = torch.tensor(discounted_rewards)
        discounted_rewards = (discounted_rewards -
discounted_rewards.mean()) / (discounted_rewards.std() + 1e-9)

        # Calculate policy loss
        policy_loss = []
        for log_prob, reward in zip(log_probs, discounted_rewards):
            policy_loss.append(-log_prob * reward)
        policy_loss = torch.cat(policy_loss).sum()

        # Update policy network
        optimizer.zero_grad()
        policy_loss.backward()
        optimizer.step()

        if (episode + 1) % 50 == 0:
            print(f"Episode {episode+1}, Total Reward: {sum(rewards)}")

train_policy(episodes=500)
env.close()
```

Explanation:
- Policy Network: A simple neural network that outputs a probability distribution over actions.
- select_action Function: Samples an action based on the policy network's output and returns the log probability for later loss computation.
- Training Loop: Runs multiple episodes where the agent collects rewards and log probabilities. The REINFORCE algorithm computes the discounted reward for each step, normalizes it, and then updates the policy network using gradient descent.
- Policy Loss: Negative log probabilities weighted by the discounted rewards, which are then minimized to improve the policy.

4.4 Multi-Agent Systems and Distributed Decision Making

While many AI systems involve a single autonomous agent, real-world applications often require multiple agents to work together. Multi-Agent Systems (MAS) consist of several interacting agents that may cooperate, compete, or operate independently within the same environment.

Key Concepts in Multi-Agent Systems
- Cooperative Agents: Work together to achieve a common goal.
- Competitive Agents: Have conflicting objectives and may compete for resources.
- Mixed Environments: Contain both cooperative and competitive interactions.
- Communication Protocols: Mechanisms by which agents share information to coordinate their actions.

Advantages of Distributed Decision Making
- Scalability: Multiple agents can cover larger areas or handle more complex tasks.
- Robustness: The failure of one agent does not incapacitate the entire system.
- Flexibility: Agents can dynamically adapt roles based on the environment.

Comparative Table: Single-Agent vs. Multi-Agent Systems

Aspect	Single-Agent Systems	Multi-Agent Systems
Complexity	Lower complexity, centralized decision-making	Higher complexity due to interactions and coordination
Scalability	Limited to one agent's capacity	Scalable by adding more agents

Robustness	Vulnerable to single point failures	More robust; redundancy allows continued operation
Coordination	No need for inter-agent communication	Requires protocols and strategies for effective collaboration

Example: Pseudocode for a Simple Multi-Agent Interaction

Below is a simplified pseudocode example that demonstrates how multiple agents might share information and make distributed decisions:

python

Copy code

```python
# Define a simple Agent class
class Agent:
    def __init__(self, id):
        self.id = id
        self.state = None  # Current state of the agent
        self.policy = None  # Decision-making strategy

    def perceive(self, environment):
        # Agent updates its state based on the environment
        self.state = environment.get_state(self.id)

    def decide(self):
        # Make a decision based on its policy (for simplicity, return a random action)
        action = "action_" + str(self.id)
        return action

    def communicate(self, other_agents):
        # Share relevant information with other agents
        shared_info = {"id": self.id, "state": self.state}
        return shared_info

# Simulate multi-agent decision-making
agents = [Agent(id=i) for i in range(3)]
environment = ...  # Assume some environment object is defined

# Each agent perceives the environment and decides on an action
for agent in agents:
```

```
agent.perceive(environment)
action = agent.decide()
print(f"Agent {agent.id} decided on {action}")

# Agents communicate with each other to coordinate decisions
communications = [agent.communicate(agents) for agent in agents]
for info in communications:
    print(f"Agent {info['id']} shares its state: {info['state']}")
```

Explanation:

- Agent Class: Defines basic functions for perceiving the environment, making a decision, and communicating with other agents.
- Multi-Agent Interaction: Each agent updates its state, makes a decision, and then shares its state with others. In a real system, this communication would be used to coordinate actions and optimize overall performance.

Summary

In Chapter 4, we explored the multifaceted nature of autonomous decision-making in AI:

- Defining Autonomy: We clarified key concepts and terminology that underpin the notion of autonomous systems.
- Decision-Making Frameworks: We compared rule-based, learning-based, and hybrid approaches, highlighting their respective strengths and limitations.
- Reinforcement Learning and Policy Optimization: We provided a detailed explanation of RL concepts, including a complete REINFORCE code example to illustrate policy optimization in practice.
- Multi-Agent Systems: We examined how distributed decision-making enables multiple agents to work together, and provided pseudocode to demonstrate basic inter-agent communication and coordination.

This comprehensive treatment equips you with both the theoretical foundation and practical tools needed to implement autonomous decision-making systems in diverse AI applications.

Chapter 5: Architecting Agentic RAG Systems

In this chapter, we focus on designing and building Agentic RAG systems that are modular, scalable, robust, and continuously adaptive. We break down the architecture into clear components and explain how each part contributes to the overall functionality of the system. We also provide code examples and tables that illustrate the key concepts.

5.1 Design Principles and Modular Architectures

Core Design Principles

When architecting an Agentic RAG system, the following design principles are paramount:

- Modularity:
  Break down the system into distinct, self-contained modules (e.g., retrieval, generation, decision-making). This separation of concerns makes the system easier to develop, test, and maintain.
- Separation of Concerns:
  Each module should have a well-defined responsibility. For example, the retrieval module focuses solely on fetching relevant information, while the generative module focuses on creating text outputs.
- Scalability:
  The architecture should support growth in data volume and user load by allowing modules to be distributed or replicated as needed.
- Flexibility and Extensibility:
  Design the system so that new components (e.g., additional decision-making strategies) can be integrated without overhauling the entire system.
- Robustness and Fault Tolerance:
  Ensure that the failure of one component does not bring down the entire system. Use error handling, redundancy, and monitoring to maintain system reliability.
- Real-Time Processing:
  For applications that require immediate responses, design the system to process data and make decisions in real time.

Modular Architecture Overview

Below is a simplified table summarizing the key modules in an Agentic RAG system and their responsibilities:

Module	Responsibility	Key Considerations
Retrieval Module	Fetch relevant external data based on user queries	Fast indexing, high recall, semantic matching

Generative Module	Generate coherent responses integrating retrieved context	Language model performance, context integration
Decision Engine	Determine the best action or strategy using input from retrieval/gener ation	Autonomous policy, reinforcement learning methods
Feedback Loop	Collect performance data and user feedback to adjust system behavior	Continuous learning, monitoring, adaptation

Example: Modular Code Structure

A simple Python class structure can illustrate how to separate concerns. Each module is defined as a class with its own methods:

python

Copy code

```python
# Retrieval Module
class RetrievalModule:
    def __init__(self, corpus):
        self.corpus = corpus  # Assume corpus is a list of documents

    def retrieve(self, query):
        # Basic keyword matching for demonstration purposes
        results = [doc for doc in self.corpus if any(word.lower() in doc.lower()
for word in query.split())]
        return results

# Generative Module
class GenerativeModule:
    def __init__(self, model):
        self.model = model  # This could be a pre-loaded transformer model

    def generate(self, query, context):
        # For simplicity, we concatenate the query and context.
```

```python
    # A real model would process these inputs to generate text.
    input_text = query + " " + " ".join(context)
    # Simulate generation; in practice, call self.model.generate(input_text)
    response = f"Generated response based on: {input_text}"
    return response


# Decision Engine
class DecisionEngine:
    def decide(self, retrieved_docs):
        # Simple decision logic based on document count
        if len(retrieved_docs) > 2:
            return "generate_detailed_response"
        else:
            return "request_more_info"


# Agentic RAG System Integrator
class AgenticRAGSystem:
    def __init__(self, corpus, model):
        self.retrieval_module = RetrievalModule(corpus)
        self.generative_module = GenerativeModule(model)
        self.decision_engine = DecisionEngine()

    def process_query(self, query):
        # Step 1: Retrieve context
        retrieved_docs = self.retrieval_module.retrieve(query)
        # Step 2: Decide on the action based on retrieved data
        decision = self.decision_engine.decide(retrieved_docs)
        # Step 3: Generate the final response
        if decision == "generate_detailed_response":
            response = self.generative_module.generate(query, retrieved_docs)
        else:
            response = "Could you please provide more details?"
        return response

# Example usage
corpus = [
    "AI is evolving rapidly with hybrid architectures.",
    "Retrieval methods enhance generative models by grounding responses
in data.",
    "Decision engines allow autonomous adjustments based on context.",
    "Scalability and real-time processing are key in modern AI systems."
```

```
]
dummy_model = None  # Placeholder for an actual language model

agentic_rag = AgenticRAGSystem(corpus, dummy_model)
query = "Tell me about AI systems with retrieval and decision making."
print("Final Response:", agentic_rag.process_query(query))
```

Explanation:
- The RetrievalModule class filters a list of documents based on a simple keyword match.
- The GenerativeModule class simulates generating a response by concatenating the query and context.
- The DecisionEngine class chooses whether to generate a detailed response or ask for more information based on the number of retrieved documents.
- The AgenticRAGSystem class integrates these modules into a unified pipeline that processes a query step by step.

5.2 Integrating Retrieval, Generation, and Decision Engines

Integration Strategy

The effective integration of the three core engines—retrieval, generation, and decision—is the backbone of an Agentic RAG system. Integration involves:
- Data Flow Coordination:
  Ensuring that the output of the retrieval module is correctly formatted and passed to both the decision engine and the generative module.
- Modular Interfaces:
  Defining clear interfaces (APIs) for each module to facilitate communication between components. This may include standardized data formats (e.g., JSON) or in-memory data structures.
- Synchronous vs. Asynchronous Processing:
  Depending on the application requirements, you may choose to integrate modules synchronously (step-by-step processing) or asynchronously (parallel processing with queues).

Example Integration Flow

Below is an expanded version of the previous code example that demonstrates the integration process:

python
Copy code
```
# Expanded AgenticRAGSystem with explicit integration steps
```

```python
class AgenticRAGSystem:
    def __init__(self, corpus, model):
        self.retrieval_module = RetrievalModule(corpus)
        self.generative_module = GenerativeModule(model)
        self.decision_engine = DecisionEngine()

    def process_query(self, query):
        # 1. Retrieve context
        print("Retrieving relevant documents...")
        retrieved_docs = self.retrieval_module.retrieve(query)
        print("Retrieved Documents:", retrieved_docs)

        # 2. Decision Engine: Determine processing strategy
        decision = self.decision_engine.decide(retrieved_docs)
        print("Decision Engine Output:", decision)

        # 3. Generation: Produce a response based on the decision
        if decision == "generate_detailed_response":
            response = self.generative_module.generate(query, retrieved_docs)
        else:
            response = "Could you please provide more details?"

        return response

# Example usage remains the same
print("Final Integrated Response:", agentic_rag.process_query(query))
```

Explanation:
- This code adds print statements to log each integration step, helping developers and readers understand the data flow and decision-making process.
- It emphasizes clear, sequential integration of the retrieval, decision, and generation components.

5.3 Scalability, Robustness, and Real-Time Processing

Scalability
Scalability ensures that the system can handle increased loads—both in terms of data and user requests. Key strategies include:

- Distributed Architectures:
  Use microservices to deploy each module on separate servers or containers. This enables horizontal scaling.
- Load Balancing:
  Implement load balancers to distribute incoming queries evenly across multiple instances of the retrieval and generative modules.
- Caching:
  Use caching mechanisms (e.g., Redis) to store frequently accessed data or computation results.

Robustness

Robustness focuses on the system's ability to handle errors and unexpected conditions gracefully:
- Error Handling:
  Implement comprehensive try-catch blocks and fallback mechanisms. For example, if the retrieval module fails, the system can either use a default context or alert the user.
- Monitoring and Logging:
  Deploy monitoring tools (e.g., Prometheus, Grafana) to track system health and performance. Detailed logs help diagnose issues quickly.
- Redundancy:
  Use redundant components so that a failure in one module does not lead to system-wide downtime.

Real-Time Processing

Real-time processing is critical for applications that require immediate responses:
- Low-Latency Communication:
  Optimize data pipelines and network configurations to minimize latency.
- Asynchronous Processing:
  Use asynchronous programming or event-driven architectures (e.g., Apache Kafka) to handle high volumes of requests concurrently.

Comparative Table

Aspect	Strategy/Technique	Benefits
Scalability	Distributed architectures, load balancing, caching	Handles increased load efficiently
Robustness	Error handling, monitoring, redundancy	Improves reliability and fault tolerance

| Real-Time Processing | Low-latency communication, asynchronous processing | Ensures timely responses and high throughput |

5.4 Feedback Loops and Continuous Learning

The Role of Feedback

Feedback loops are essential for creating systems that learn and adapt over time. They enable the Agentic RAG system to:

- Monitor Performance:
  Continuously collect data on the quality of generated responses and user interactions.
- Refine Decisions:
  Use performance metrics and user feedback to adjust decision-making policies.
- Improve Models:
  Update retrieval indexes, fine-tune generative models, or adjust reinforcement learning parameters based on observed outcomes.

Implementing Feedback Loops

A typical feedback loop involves:

1. Data Collection:
   Logging system performance, user feedback, and error rates.
2. Analysis:
   Processing the collected data to identify patterns, errors, or opportunities for improvement.
3. Model Update:
   Applying machine learning techniques (e.g., online learning or periodic retraining) to update system components.
4. Deployment:
   Rolling out updated models or policies in a controlled manner.

Example: Pseudocode for a Feedback Loop

Below is a simplified pseudocode example that demonstrates a feedback loop integrated within the system:

python

Copy code

```python
def collect_feedback(response, user_rating):
    """
    Simulate feedback collection from users.
    """
    # For demonstration, we log the response and a user rating (1-5)
```

```python
    feedback_entry = {"response": response, "rating": user_rating}
    return feedback_entry

def update_model_based_on_feedback(feedback_list):
    """
    Process feedback and update models/policies.
    In practice, this might involve retraining or fine-tuning a model.
    """
    average_rating = sum(feedback["rating"] for feedback in feedback_list) / len(feedback_list)
    print(f"Average User Rating: {average_rating:.2f}")
    if average_rating < 3:
        print("Triggering model review and update...")
        # Insert model update logic here
    else:
        print("Model performance is satisfactory.")

# Simulate feedback loop usage
feedback_list = []
response = agentic_rag.process_query("What is hybrid AI?")
print("Initial Response:", response)
feedback_list.append(collect_feedback(response, user_rating=4))
feedback_list.append(collect_feedback(response, user_rating=2))
update_model_based_on_feedback(feedback_list)
```

Explanation:
- collect_feedback: This function simulates user feedback collection.
- update_model_based_on_feedback: Computes an average rating and triggers an update if the performance is below a certain threshold.
- In a production environment, feedback data would be collected continuously and used to retrain models or adjust decision policies.

Summary

In Chapter 5, we explored the architectural design of Agentic RAG systems with a focus on:
- Design Principles and Modular Architectures:
  We emphasized modularity, separation of concerns, scalability, and robustness. A table and code examples illustrated how to structure the system into distinct modules.

- Integrating Retrieval, Generation, and Decision Engines:
  We demonstrated the integration of these core components through clear data flow and a sample code pipeline that connects each module.
- Scalability, Robustness, and Real-Time Processing:
  Strategies such as distributed architectures, load balancing, error handling, and asynchronous processing were discussed and summarized in a comparative table.
- Feedback Loops and Continuous Learning:
  We explained the importance of feedback in adapting system performance over time, including pseudocode that outlines a basic feedback loop.

This comprehensive approach provides you with a solid foundation for designing, implementing, and optimizing Agentic RAG systems that are not only effective today but also adaptable to future challenges and innovations.

Chapter 6: Data Pipelines and Preprocessing for Agentic RAG

Data forms the foundation of any AI system, and for Agentic RAG, well-structured data pipelines and thorough preprocessing are critical. This chapter covers strategies for collecting and curating data, methods for cleaning, normalizing, and augmenting data, solutions for indexing and storage, and practices to ensure data integrity while mitigating bias. By following these guidelines, you can build a robust, efficient, and fair data infrastructure for your Agentic RAG system.

6.1 Data Collection and Curation Strategies

Overview

The first step in building any data-driven system is gathering the right data from reliable sources. For Agentic RAG systems, data can come from various sources such as:

- Public datasets (e.g., academic repositories, news articles)
- Web scraping of online content
- APIs provided by organizations (e.g., social media, government, financial data)
- Internal databases or proprietary sources

Data Collection Strategies

1. Web Scraping:
   Automate the extraction of data from websites using tools like Python's BeautifulSoup or Scrapy.
2. APIs:
   Use RESTful or GraphQL APIs to collect structured data from online services. Many organizations provide API endpoints for accessing up-to-date information.
3. Public Datasets:
   Leverage publicly available datasets from sources like Kaggle, UCI Machine Learning Repository, or government databases.
4. User-Generated Data:
   Collect data directly from users through forms, surveys, or interaction logs if applicable.

Data Curation

Curation involves selecting, organizing, and maintaining data to ensure it is useful for your application. Key steps include:

- Filtering:
  Remove irrelevant or duplicate entries to maintain quality.
- Labeling:
  Annotate data where necessary (e.g., tagging topics or sentiment) to facilitate downstream processing.

- Versioning:
  Keep track of data updates and changes using version control systems or data management tools.

Example: Simple Web Scraping Script

Below is a Python code example using BeautifulSoup to scrape headlines from a news website:

Pythian

Copy code

```
import requests
from bs4 import BeautifulSoup

def scrape_headlines(url):
    """
    Scrape headlines from the specified URL.
    """
    response = requests.get(url)
    soup = BeautifulSoup(response.content, 'html.parser')
    headlines = [h.get_text(strip=True) for h in soup.find_all('h2')]
    return headlines

# Example usage:
news_url = 'https://example-news-site.com'
headlines = scrape_headlines(news_url)
print("Scraped Headlines:")
for headline in headlines:
    print("-", headline)
```

Explanation:
- requests.get: Fetches the webpage content.
- BeautifulSoup: Parses HTML content.
- find_all('h2'): Assumes that headlines are wrapped in <h2> tags.
- The code collects and prints the headlines.

6.2 Cleaning, Normalization, and Augmentation Techniques

Data Cleaning

Data cleaning is the process of detecting and correcting (or removing) errors and inconsistencies in data. Typical cleaning tasks include:
- Removing Noise:
  Eliminate irrelevant characters, punctuation, or HTML tags.

- Handling Missing Values:
  Fill in or remove missing data points.
- Deduplication:
  Remove duplicate entries to prevent bias in model training.

Data Normalization

Normalization involves transforming data into a common format:

- Text Normalization:
  Convert text to lowercase, remove special characters, and perform stemming or lemmatization.
- Numerical Normalization:
  Scale numerical features using techniques like min-max scaling or z-score normalization.

Data Augmentation

Augmentation techniques generate new data samples from existing ones to improve model robustness:

- Text Augmentation:
  Techniques such as synonym replacement, random insertion, or back-translation.
- Image Augmentation:
  If working with visual data, perform rotations, flips, or color adjustments.

Example: Text Cleaning with Python

The following Python example uses the nltk library to clean and normalize text data:

python

Copy code

```python
import re
import nltk
from nltk.corpus import stopwords
from nltk.stem import WordNetLemmatizer

# Download required resources
nltk.download('stopwords')
nltk.download('wordnet')

def clean_text(text):
    """
    Clean and normalize text by:
    - Lowercasing
    - Removing punctuation and numbers
    - Removing stopwords
    - Lemmatizing words
    """

    # Lowercase the text
```

```python
    text = text.lower()
    # Remove punctuation and numbers
    text = re.sub(r'[^a-z\s]', '', text)
    # Tokenize text
    words = text.split()
    # Remove stopwords
    stop_words = set(stopwords.words('english'))
    words = [word for word in words if word not in stop_words]
    # Lemmatize words
    lemmatizer = WordNetLemmatizer()
    words = [lemmatizer.lemmatize(word) for word in words]
    # Join words back into a single string
    return ' '.join(words)

# Example usage:
raw_text = "Agentic RAG systems are revolutionizing AI! They integrate
retrieval & generation seamlessly."
cleaned_text = clean_text(raw_text)
print("Cleaned Text:", cleaned_text)
```

Explanation:
- Lowercasing: Ensures uniformity.
- Regular Expressions: Remove punctuation and numbers.
- Stopwords Removal: Filters out common words that add little value.
- Lemmatization: Converts words to their base form.

6.3 Indexing and Efficient Storage Solutions

Indexing Strategies
Efficient retrieval of data relies on well-designed indexing:
- Inverted Index:
  Commonly used for text retrieval, where each term maps to its locations in the corpus.
- Vector Indexing:
  Techniques such as FAISS (Facebook AI Similarity Search) enable fast similarity search in high-dimensional spaces using vector embeddings.
- Database Indexes:
  Use database indexing (e.g., B-tree indexes in SQL databases) for structured data.

Storage Solutions
Efficient storage is essential for handling large volumes of data:

- Relational Databases (SQL):
  Suitable for structured data with complex relationships.
- NoSQL Databases:
  Options like MongoDB or Cassandra work well for semi-structured or unstructured data.
- Distributed File Systems:
  Systems such as Hadoop HDFS or cloud storage solutions (e.g., AWS S3) enable scalable storage of large datasets.

Comparative Table

Technique/ Tool	Type	Use Case	Key Benefits
Inverted Index	Text Retrieval	Fast keyword search in document corpora	High-speed lookup, low memory footprint
FAISS	Vector Indexing	Similarity search for dense embeddings	Efficient for high-dimensional data
Relational Databases (SQL)	Structured Storage	Storing structured, relational data	ACID compliance, complex queries
NoSQL Databases	Unstructure d Storage	Handling large-scale, flexible schema data	High scalability, flexible data models

Example: Building a Simple Inverted Index

Below is a Python code example that builds a basic inverted index for a small corpus:

python

Copy code

```
from collections import defaultdict

def build_inverted_index(corpus):
    """
    Build an inverted index from a corpus.
    corpus: list of strings, where each string represents a document.
    Returns a dictionary where keys are words and values are sets of
document indices.
    """
    index = defaultdict(set)
```

```
    for doc_id, document in enumerate(corpus):
        words = document.lower().split()
        for word in words:
            index[word].add(doc_id)
    return index

# Example corpus
corpus = [
    "Agentic RAG systems integrate retrieval and generation.",
    "Retrieval modules help to fetch relevant information.",
    "Generative models create coherent text responses."
]

inverted_index = build_inverted_index(corpus)
print("Inverted Index:")
for word, doc_ids in inverted_index.items():
    print(f"{word}: {sorted(list(doc_ids))}")
```

Explanation:
- build_inverted_index: Iterates through each document, tokenizes text, and maps each word to the document IDs in which it appears.
- defaultdict(set): Efficiently aggregates document IDs for each word.

6.4 Ensuring Data Integrity and Mitigating Bias

Data Integrity

Data integrity ensures that data is accurate, consistent, and reliable over its lifecycle:
- Validation:
  Implement data validation rules at the point of collection to prevent corrupt or malformed data.
- Consistency Checks:
  Regularly perform checksums or hash comparisons to ensure data has not been altered unexpectedly.
- Version Control:
  Use data versioning to track changes and enable rollback if needed.

Mitigating Bias

Bias in data can lead to skewed or unfair outcomes in AI systems. Strategies to mitigate bias include:

- Diverse Data Sources:
  Collect data from multiple sources to avoid over-representation of a particular perspective.
- Bias Detection:
  Use statistical tests and visualization techniques to identify potential biases in your dataset.
- Preprocessing Adjustments:
  Apply techniques such as re-sampling, re-weighting, or adversarial debiasing to correct imbalances.

Example: Simple Data Integrity Check

Below is a Python code example that demonstrates how to perform a basic integrity check using hash functions:

python

Copy code

```python
import hashlib

def compute_hash(text):
    """
    Compute the SHA-256 hash of a given text string.
    """
    return hashlib.sha256(text.encode('utf-8')).hexdigest()

# Example usage:
data_entry = "Agentic RAG systems integrate retrieval with autonomous decision-making."
data_hash = compute_hash(data_entry)
print("Data Entry Hash:", data_hash)

# Integrity check: Compare the stored hash with a newly computed hash
stored_hash = data_hash  # In practice, this would be stored securely
new_hash = compute_hash(data_entry)
if new_hash == stored_hash:
    print("Data integrity verified.")
else:
    print("Data integrity compromised.")
```

Explanation:
- compute_hash: Uses SHA-256 to create a unique fingerprint of the data.
- Integrity Check: Compares a stored hash with a newly computed one to verify that the data has not been altered.

Addressing Bias: A Practical Approach

Consider a scenario where your text data may over-represent one viewpoint. You might:

- Analyze Word Distributions:
  Visualize word frequency across different demographic groups.
- Re-Sample Data:
  Adjust the dataset to include a more balanced representation.

While a full implementation is beyond the scope of this chapter, numerous libraries (such as Fairlearn for machine learning fairness) can help diagnose and mitigate bias.

Summary

In Chapter 6, we explored the essential components of building robust data pipelines for Agentic RAG systems:

- Data Collection and Curation Strategies:
  We discussed various methods for gathering data—from web scraping and APIs to public datasets—and outlined key curation practices.
- Cleaning, Normalization, and Augmentation Techniques:
  We covered processes for preparing raw data, including cleaning, normalizing text, and augmenting datasets to improve model performance.
- Indexing and Efficient Storage Solutions:
  We reviewed strategies for indexing (e.g., inverted indexes, vector indexing) and summarized storage solutions with a comparative table and example code.
- Ensuring Data Integrity and Mitigating Bias:
  We examined techniques for verifying data accuracy using hash functions and discussed approaches for reducing bias in data pipelines.

By following these practices, you will ensure that your Agentic RAG system is built on a foundation of high-quality, reliable, and fair data, enabling it to generate accurate and contextually rich responses.

Chapter 7: Building the Retrieval Module

In an Agentic RAG system, the retrieval module is responsible for identifying and returning relevant pieces of information from a large corpus or database. A well-designed retrieval module ensures that the generative component receives accurate and contextually rich data to integrate into its responses. In this chapter, we cover:

1. Overview of Retrieval Methods: A look at traditional and neural approaches.
2. Advanced Indexing Algorithms and Similarity Metrics: How to efficiently index data and measure relevance.
3. Integration with Search Engines and Databases: Connecting the retrieval module with external data sources.
4. Performance Optimization for Speed and Accuracy: Techniques to ensure the retrieval module meets real-time and accuracy requirements.

7.1 Overview of Retrieval Methods: Traditional and Neural Approaches

Retrieval methods are central to finding relevant documents or data points from a large corpus. Broadly, these methods can be categorized into:

Traditional Retrieval Methods

Traditional approaches rely on lexical matching and statistical models. Common techniques include:

- Keyword Matching: Searches for exact matches of the query words in documents.
- TF-IDF (Term Frequency-Inverse Document Frequency): Weighs terms based on their frequency in a document relative to the corpus.
- BM25: A probabilistic retrieval model that ranks documents using term frequency, document length, and saturation parameters.

These methods are efficient, easy to implement, and work well when queries are specific and the vocabulary is limited.

Neural Retrieval Methods

Neural methods use deep learning to capture semantic meaning rather than just exact word matches. Key approaches include:

- Dense Embedding Models: These models (e.g., Sentence-BERT) encode both queries and documents into dense vector representations. Similarity is then measured in the embedding space.
- Dual Encoder Architectures: Separate neural networks encode queries and documents; a similarity metric (often cosine similarity) is used for matching.
- Cross-Encoders: Process both query and document together, typically resulting in more precise (but computationally expensive) relevance scores.

Comparative Overview

Method	Approach	Pros	Cons
Keyword Matching	Lexical matching	Simple, fast, easy to implement	Limited by vocabulary; ignores context
TF-IDF / BM25	Statistical weighting	Effective for many text retrieval tasks	Does not capture semantic meaning
Dense Embeddings	Neural semantic encoding	Captures context and meaning, robust	Requires substantial compute and training data
Dual/Cross-Encoders	Neural matching	High accuracy, contextual relevance	More computationall y intensive

7.2 Advanced Indexing Algorithms and Similarity Metrics

To retrieve information quickly and accurately, efficient indexing and effective similarity metrics are essential.

Advanced Indexing Algorithms

1. Inverted Index:
   A fundamental data structure for text retrieval that maps each term to the documents in which it appears.
2. Vector Indexing:
   Used for dense embeddings. Libraries such as FAISS (Facebook AI Similarity Search) allow for efficient approximate nearest neighbor (ANN) searches in high-dimensional spaces.
3. Hybrid Indexing:
   Combines lexical (e.g., BM25) and semantic (e.g., dense vector search) methods for improved performance.

Similarity Metrics

The choice of similarity metric is crucial in ranking retrieved documents:

- Cosine Similarity:
  Measures the cosine of the angle between two vectors. Particularly useful for dense embeddings.

- Euclidean Distance:
  Calculates the straight-line distance between two points in space. Less common for text embeddings but still applicable.
- Dot Product:
  Can be used in models where the magnitude of vectors also carries meaning.

Code Example: Cosine Similarity with Dense Embeddings

Below is a Python example using NumPy to calculate cosine similarity between a query embedding and document embeddings.

python

Copy code

```python
import numpy as np
from sklearn.metrics.pairwise import cosine_similarity

def compute_cosine_similarity(query_vec, doc_vecs):
    """
    Compute cosine similarity between a query vector and a list of document vectors.
    Returns the similarity scores as a numpy array.
    """
    # Reshape query_vec to 2D array for compatibility with cosine_similarity function
    query_vec = query_vec.reshape(1, -1)
    similarities = cosine_similarity(query_vec, doc_vecs)
    return similarities.flatten()

# Example embeddings (for demonstration)
query_embedding = np.array([0.5, 0.1, 0.3])
document_embeddings = np.array([
    [0.4, 0.2, 0.4],
    [0.1, 0.3, 0.2],
    [0.5, 0.0, 0.3]
])

similarity_scores = compute_cosine_similarity(query_embedding, document_embeddings)
print("Cosine Similarity Scores:", similarity_scores)
```

Explanation:
- The function compute_cosine_similarity reshapes the query vector and computes cosine similarity with a set of document vectors.
- The output is a list of similarity scores, which can be used to rank the documents.

7.3 Integration with Search Engines and Databases

Integrating the retrieval module with external search engines and databases is critical for scaling and leveraging existing infrastructure.

Integration Approaches

1. Direct API Integration:
   Many search engines (e.g., Elasticsearch, Solr) provide RESTful APIs. Your retrieval module can send a query and receive a ranked list of documents.
2. Database Querying:
   Structured data in SQL or NoSQL databases can be queried using standard query languages (SQL, MongoDB query language). Indexing strategies (like B-tree indexes) enhance query performance.
3. Hybrid Integration:
   Combine search engine results with internal retrieval processes. For example, you can use Elasticsearch to quickly narrow down candidates and then apply a neural re-ranking model on the results.

Example: Querying Elasticsearch from Python

Below is a Python code snippet demonstrating how to query Elasticsearch using the official Python client.

python

Copy code

```python
from elasticsearch import Elasticsearch

# Initialize the Elasticsearch client (assumes Elasticsearch is running locally)
es = Elasticsearch([{'host': 'localhost', 'port': 9200}])

def search_elasticsearch(index, query, size=5):
    """
    Query the specified Elasticsearch index and return the top documents.
    """
    search_body = {
        "query": {
            "match": {
                "content": query
            }
        },
        "size": size
    }
```

```
response = es.search(index=index, body=search_body)
results = [hit['_source']['content'] for hit in response['hits']['hits']]
return results

# Example usage:
index_name = "documents"
query_text = "autonomous decision making"
results = search_elasticsearch(index_name, query_text)
print("Elasticsearch Results:")
for result in results:
    print("-", result)
```

Explanation:
- Elasticsearch Client: Initializes a connection to a local Elasticsearch instance.
- search_elasticsearch Function: Constructs a query using a match query on the "content" field and retrieves the top results.
- This demonstrates how external search engines can be seamlessly integrated into your retrieval module.

7.4 Performance Optimization for Speed and Accuracy

Performance is critical in retrieval systems, especially when operating in real-time environments. Here are several strategies to optimize both speed and accuracy.

Techniques for Speed Optimization
1. Caching:
   Use in-memory caching (e.g., Redis) to store frequent query results, reducing the need for repeated processing.
2. Parallel Processing:
   Distribute the retrieval workload across multiple processors or servers using parallel computing frameworks.
3. Approximate Nearest Neighbor (ANN) Search:
   Use libraries like FAISS to perform ANN searches, which offer a good trade-off between speed and accuracy for high-dimensional vectors.
4. Efficient Data Structures:
   Use optimized data structures such as inverted indexes and balanced trees to speed up query processing.

Techniques for Accuracy Optimization
1. Hybrid Ranking:
   Combine multiple retrieval methods (e.g., BM25 with dense vector search) to improve ranking quality.

2. Re-Ranking:
   Apply a secondary re-ranking step using a more sophisticated neural model to refine the initial results.
3. Hyperparameter Tuning:
   Optimize parameters such as the number of nearest neighbors, weighting factors in BM25, and embedding dimensions to balance performance and accuracy.

Comparative Table

Optimization Aspect	Technique	Benefits
Speed	Caching, Parallel Processing	Reduces response times, handles high loads
Speed	Approximate Nearest Neighbor (ANN)	Efficient retrieval in high-dimensional space
Accuracy	Hybrid Ranking	Leverages strengths of multiple methods
Accuracy	Re-Ranking	Improves precision of final results

Example: Using FAISS for Fast Vector Search

Below is an example of how to use FAISS to perform an approximate nearest neighbor search on dense vectors.

python

Copy code

```python
import numpy as np
import faiss

# Create a random dataset of embeddings (e.g., 1000 documents, 64-dimensional embeddings)
d = 64  # Dimension of embeddings
nb = 1000  # Number of database vectors
np.random.seed(123)
database_vectors = np.random.random((nb, d)).astype('float32')

# Build the FAISS index
index = faiss.IndexFlatL2(d)  # L2 distance index
index.add(database_vectors)
print(f"Number of vectors indexed: {index.ntotal}")
```

```
# Query: generate a random query vector
query_vector = np.random.random((1, d)).astype('float32')

# Perform a search for the top 5 nearest neighbors
k = 5
distances, indices = index.search(query_vector, k)
print("Top 5 nearest neighbors:")
for i, (idx, dist) in enumerate(zip(indices[0], distances[0])):
    print(f"{i + 1}: Document ID {idx} with distance {dist:.4f}")
```

Explanation:
- FAISS Index: The code creates an index for 64-dimensional vectors using L2 distance.
- Indexing and Search: Vectors are added to the index, and a query vector is used to retrieve the top 5 closest vectors.
- This demonstrates a practical method to achieve fast and scalable vector search.

Summary
In Chapter 7, we delved into building an effective retrieval module for Agentic RAG systems:
- Overview of Retrieval Methods: We discussed traditional approaches (keyword matching, TF-IDF, BM25) and neural methods (dense embeddings, dual encoders), including their advantages and disadvantages.
- Advanced Indexing and Similarity Metrics: We examined techniques such as inverted and vector indexing, and explored metrics like cosine similarity with a complete code example.
- Integration with External Systems: We provided examples of integrating with search engines like Elasticsearch and discussed strategies for querying databases.
- Performance Optimization: We reviewed various techniques to improve speed and accuracy, including caching, parallel processing, and the use of FAISS for approximate nearest neighbor search.

By implementing these strategies, you can build a robust, efficient, and accurate retrieval module that forms the backbone of your Agentic RAG system.

Chapter 8: Developing the Generative Component

In an Agentic RAG system, the generative component is responsible for creating coherent, contextually relevant, and high-quality text responses. This chapter covers the latest advancements in language generation models, effective training and fine-tuning strategies, methods to evaluate the quality of generated text, and techniques for managing context and controlling the output. These insights will help you build a robust generative engine that meets both performance and quality standards.

8.1 Advances in Language Generation: Transformer Models and Beyond

The Rise of Transformer Models

Over the past few years, transformer models have revolutionized natural language processing (NLP) by introducing the self-attention mechanism, which allows models to capture long-range dependencies in text more effectively than previous architectures such as RNNs or LSTMs. Key developments include:

- BERT (Bidirectional Encoder Representations from Transformers):
  Primarily designed for understanding language, BERT reads text bidirectionally, making it highly effective for tasks like question answering and sentiment analysis.
- GPT (Generative Pre-trained Transformer):
  GPT models, including GPT-2 and GPT-3, are designed for text generation. They predict the next word in a sequence, allowing them to generate coherent and contextually rich text.
- T5 (Text-to-Text Transfer Transformer):
  A versatile model that frames all NLP tasks as text-to-text problems, enabling a unified approach to tasks ranging from translation to summarization.

Beyond Transformers

Recent research is expanding on the transformer framework with improvements such as:

- Long-Range Transformers:
  Variants designed to handle longer contexts by reducing the quadratic complexity of self-attention (e.g., Longformer, BigBird).
- Efficient Transformers:
  Models that optimize computational efficiency and memory usage without sacrificing performance (e.g., Reformer, Linformer).

Comparative Overview

Model	Primary Focus	Strengths	Limitations

BERT	Language understanding	Excellent for comprehension tasks	Not primarily designed for text generation
GPT Series	Text generation	Generates coherent, context-rich text	May produce less factual content without retrieval
T5	Text-to-text tasks	Versatile across many NLP tasks	Can be computationally intensive
Long-Range Transformers	Extended context handling	Efficient for longer sequences	May require specialized training or hardware
Efficient Transformers	Resource optimization	Lower memory and compute requirements	Sometimes trade off accuracy for speed

Example: Text Generation with Hugging Face's Transformers

Below is a simple Python example using Hugging Face's Transformers library to generate text with a GPT-2 model:

python

Copy code

```python
from transformers import GPT2LMHeadModel, GPT2Tokenizer

# Load pre-trained GPT-2 model and tokenizer
model_name = 'gpt2'
tokenizer = GPT2Tokenizer.from_pretrained(model_name)
model = GPT2LMHeadModel.from_pretrained(model_name)

# Prepare input text
input_text = "Agentic RAG systems revolutionize AI by"
input_ids = tokenizer.encode(input_text, return_tensors='pt')

# Generate text with specified parameters
output = model.generate(
    input_ids,
    max_length=100,
    num_return_sequences=1,
    no_repeat_ngram_size=2,
```

```
    top_k=50,
    top_p=0.95,
    temperature=0.7,
    early_stopping=True
)

# Decode and print the output
generated_text = tokenizer.decode(output[0], skip_special_tokens=True)
print("Generated Text:\n", generated_text)
```

Explanation:
- The code loads a pre-trained GPT-2 model and its tokenizer.
- It encodes an initial prompt, then generates a sequence of up to 100 tokens using parameters that control repetition and randomness.
- The generated text is decoded and printed.

8.2 Training Strategies and Fine-Tuning Techniques

Pretraining and Fine-Tuning
- Pretraining:
  Large language models are first pretrained on vast amounts of text data using self-supervised objectives (e.g., next-word prediction). This step allows the model to learn general language patterns and contextual relationships.
- Fine-Tuning:
  Fine-tuning adapts the pre-trained model to specific tasks or domains by training it on a smaller, task-specific dataset. This process refines the model's abilities, making it more effective for particular applications.

Fine-Tuning Techniques
1. Supervised Fine-Tuning:
   Uses labeled datasets where the input-output relationship is explicitly provided. Common in tasks like translation or summarization.
2. Unsupervised or Self-Supervised Fine-Tuning:
   Models learn by predicting parts of the input or using masked language modeling, even in the absence of explicit labels.
3. Reinforcement Learning from Human Feedback (RLHF):
   Integrates human evaluations into the training process to better align model outputs with user expectations. This technique has been used to improve the safety and quality of models like ChatGPT.

Example: Fine-Tuning with Hugging Face Trainer API

Below is a simplified example showing how to fine-tune a transformer model using Hugging Face's Trainer API:

python
Copy code

```python
from transformers import GPT2LMHeadModel, GPT2Tokenizer, TextDataset, DataCollatorForLanguageModeling, Trainer, TrainingArguments

# Load pre-trained model and tokenizer
model_name = 'gpt2'
model = GPT2LMHeadModel.from_pretrained(model_name)
tokenizer = GPT2Tokenizer.from_pretrained(model_name)

# Prepare dataset
def load_dataset(file_path, tokenizer, block_size=128):
    return TextDataset(
        tokenizer=tokenizer,
        file_path=file_path,
        block_size=block_size
    )

train_dataset = load_dataset('train.txt', tokenizer)
data_collator = DataCollatorForLanguageModeling(tokenizer=tokenizer, mlm=False)

# Define training arguments
training_args = TrainingArguments(
    output_dir='./results',
    overwrite_output_dir=True,
    num_train_epochs=3,
    per_device_train_batch_size=4,
    save_steps=10_000,
    save_total_limit=2,
)

# Initialize Trainer
trainer = Trainer(
    model=model,
    args=training_args,
    data_collator=data_collator,
    train_dataset=train_dataset,
```

```
)

# Start fine-tuning
trainer.train()
```

Explanation:
- TextDataset: Loads a text dataset from a file.
- DataCollatorForLanguageModeling: Prepares batches for language modeling.
- TrainingArguments: Configures training parameters such as the number of epochs and batch size.
- Trainer: Combines the model, dataset, and training arguments into a high-level API for fine-tuning.

8.3 Evaluating Generation Quality: Metrics and Benchmarks

Common Evaluation Metrics
Evaluating the quality of generated text is challenging, but several metrics have become standard:
- BLEU (Bilingual Evaluation Understudy):
  Measures the overlap between the generated text and one or more reference texts. Common in machine translation.
- ROUGE (Recall-Oriented Understudy for Gisting Evaluation):
  Focuses on the recall of n-grams, often used for summarization tasks.
- Perplexity:
  Quantifies how well a probability model predicts a sample. Lower perplexity indicates better performance.
- BERTScore:
  Uses contextual embeddings to compare generated text with references, capturing semantic similarity.

Human Evaluation
Automated metrics may not fully capture aspects like fluency, coherence, and relevance. Therefore, human evaluation remains essential. Methods include:
- Rating Scales:
  Human judges rate responses on various criteria.
- Pairwise Comparisons:
  Evaluators choose the better of two generated outputs.
- Task-Based Evaluation:
  Assessing performance on downstream tasks or user satisfaction.

Comparative Table

Metric	Focus	Strengths	Limitations

BLEU	N-gram overlap	Well-established in machine translation	May not capture semantic nuances
ROUGE	Recall of n-grams	Good for summarization tasks	Can be insensitive to phrasing changes
Perplexity	Model prediction capability	Directly reflects model confidence	Lower perplexity does not always mean better human quality
BERTScore	Semantic similarity	Leverages contextual embeddings	Requires significant compute resources

Example: Calculating Perplexity

Below is a Python example that demonstrates how to compute perplexity using a pre-trained model:

python

Copy code

```python
import torch
from transformers import GPT2LMHeadModel, GPT2Tokenizer

def calculate_perplexity(text, model, tokenizer):
    """
    Calculate the perplexity of a given text using the model.
    """
    encodings = tokenizer(text, return_tensors='pt')
    max_length = model.config.n_positions
    stride = 512

    nlls = []
    for i in range(0, encodings.input_ids.size(1), stride):
        begin_loc = max(i + stride - max_length, 0)
        end_loc = i + stride
        input_ids = encodings.input_ids[:, begin_loc:end_loc]
        target_ids = input_ids.clone()
        target_ids[:, :-stride] = -100  # Mask tokens not to be predicted

        with torch.no_grad():
            outputs = model(input_ids, labels=target_ids)
            neg_log_likelihood = outputs.loss * stride
```

```
    nlls.append(neg_log_likelihood)
  ppl = torch.exp(torch.stack(nlls).sum() / end_loc)
  return ppl.item()

# Example usage:
model = GPT2LMHeadModel.from_pretrained('gpt2')
tokenizer = GPT2Tokenizer.from_pretrained('gpt2')
sample_text = "Agentic RAG systems combine retrieval and generation to
produce dynamic responses."
perplexity = calculate_perplexity(sample_text, model, tokenizer)
print("Perplexity:", perplexity)
```

Explanation:
- The function calculate_perplexity tokenizes the input text and divides it into segments.
- It computes the negative log-likelihood for each segment and aggregates the results.
- The perplexity is calculated as the exponential of the average negative log-likelihood.

8.4 Managing Context and Controlling Output

Managing Context

Language models have a finite context window, meaning they can only consider a limited number of tokens at a time. **Strategies to manage context include:**
- Truncation and Sliding Windows:
  For long texts, use a sliding window approach to process overlapping segments.
- Hierarchical Context Modeling:
  Process long documents in sections and combine the results.
- Dynamic Context Integration:
  Retrieve only the most relevant context for the query, ensuring that the generative model receives concise and pertinent information.

Controlling Output

Controlling the style, tone, and content of generated text is essential for achieving desired outcomes. Techniques include:
- Temperature Scaling:
  A lower temperature makes the model more conservative, while a higher temperature encourages more diverse outputs.

- Top-K Sampling:
  Restricts the model to sampling only from the top K most likely next tokens.
- Top-P (Nucleus) Sampling:
  Chooses tokens from the smallest set whose cumulative probability exceeds a threshold pp.
- Prompt Engineering:
  Crafting prompts carefully to steer the model toward the desired style or content.

Example: Controlling Generation with Sampling Techniques

Below is a Python example that demonstrates how to use temperature, top-k, and top-p sampling with Hugging Face's Transformers:

python

Copy code

```python
from transformers import GPT2LMHeadModel, GPT2Tokenizer

# Load model and tokenizer
model_name = 'gpt2'
tokenizer = GPT2Tokenizer.from_pretrained(model_name)
model = GPT2LMHeadModel.from_pretrained(model_name)

# Input prompt
input_text = "In the future, agentic RAG systems will"
input_ids = tokenizer.encode(input_text, return_tensors='pt')

# Generate text with controlled sampling parameters
output = model.generate(
    input_ids,
    max_length=80,
    temperature=0.8,   # Controls randomness
    top_k=40,          # Limits the candidate tokens to top 40
    top_p=0.9,         # Nucleus sampling threshold
    num_return_sequences=1,
    no_repeat_ngram_size=2,
    early_stopping=True
)

# Decode the generated text
generated_output = tokenizer.decode(output[0],
skip_special_tokens=True)
print("Controlled Generated Output:\n", generated_output)
```

Explanation:

- Temperature: Adjusts the randomness of the sampling.
- Top-K and Top-P: Control which tokens are considered during generation.
- The example demonstrates how to fine-tune these parameters to guide the model toward generating coherent and controlled text.

Summary

In Chapter 8, we explored the development of the generative component in Agentic RAG systems:

- Advances in Language Generation: We reviewed the evolution from traditional RNNs to transformer models, highlighting key architectures like GPT, BERT, and T5, along with recent innovations.
- Training Strategies and Fine-Tuning Techniques: We discussed pretraining, supervised fine-tuning, and advanced approaches such as reinforcement learning from human feedback, supported by example code using Hugging Face's Trainer API.
- Evaluating Generation Quality: We examined standard evaluation metrics (BLEU, ROUGE, perplexity, BERTScore) and the role of human evaluation, including a code example for calculating perplexity.
- Managing Context and Controlling Output: We detailed methods for handling long contexts and techniques for controlling generation output (temperature scaling, top-k, top-p sampling), with an illustrative code snippet.

Together, these sections provide a thorough understanding of how to develop, fine-tune, and evaluate a generative component that is capable of producing high-quality text, tailored to the needs of an Agentic RAG system.

Chapter 9: Integrating Autonomous Decision-Making

An essential feature of Agentic RAG systems is the ability to make autonomous decisions about how to retrieve information, generate responses, and adapt to changing environments. In this chapter, we discuss how to design a decision engine that can determine the best course of action, integrate reinforcement learning for continuous improvement, handle real-time decision making, and combine rule-based strategies with learning algorithms for a hybrid approach.

9.1 Designing the Decision Engine for Agentic RAG

Overview

The decision engine acts as the central coordinator in an Agentic RAG system. It evaluates the information retrieved from external sources and guides the generative module in producing the final output. Key responsibilities include:

- Evaluating Context: Assessing retrieved data for relevance and quality.
- Selecting Actions: Deciding whether to generate a detailed response, ask for clarification, or take alternative actions.
- Interfacing Modules: Communicating with both the retrieval and generative components.

Design Considerations

When designing the decision engine, consider the following:

- Modularity: The decision engine should be a standalone component with a clear API.
- Flexibility: It must be capable of handling different scenarios and inputs.
- Extensibility: The architecture should allow for easy integration of additional decision-making strategies in the future.

Comparative Table of Decision Engine Approaches

Aspect	Rule-Based Engine	Learning-Based Engine
Decision Logic	Predefined if-then rules	Adaptively learned policies through experience
Transparency	Highly interpretable	Often a "black box" but can be partially interpretable (e.g., via feature importance)

Flexibility	Limited to predefined scenarios	Can adapt to new, unseen situations over time
Implementation Ease	Simple to implement and test	Requires training data and careful tuning

Example: A Simple Rule-Based Decision Engine

Below is a Python example demonstrating a simple rule-based decision engine that decides whether to generate a detailed response based on the number of retrieved documents.

python

Copy code

```python
class DecisionEngine:
    def __init__(self, threshold=3):
        # threshold: minimum number of relevant documents required for a detailed response
        self.threshold = threshold

    def decide(self, retrieved_docs):
        """
        Decide the course of action based on the number of retrieved documents.
        Returns a string indicating the decision.
        """
        if len(retrieved_docs) >= self.threshold:
            return "generate_detailed_response"
        else:
            return "request_more_information"

# Example usage:
retrieved_docs_example = ["doc1", "doc2", "doc3", "doc4"]
engine = DecisionEngine(threshold=3)
decision = engine.decide(retrieved_docs_example)
print("Decision:", decision)  # Expected output: "generate_detailed_response"
```

Explanation:

- The decision engine checks whether the number of retrieved documents meets a preset threshold.

- If the threshold is met, it opts to generate a detailed response; otherwise, it requests additional information.

9.2 Incorporating Reinforcement Learning into the RAG Framework

Overview
Reinforcement Learning (RL) can be integrated into the decision engine to allow the system to improve its decision-making policy over time. In an RL framework, the decision engine (agent) interacts with its environment (the RAG system), receives feedback (rewards or penalties), and updates its policy accordingly.

Key RL Components in This Context
- State: The current situation or context, which may include metrics such as the number and quality of retrieved documents.
- Action: The decision the engine can take (e.g., generate detailed response, ask for clarification).
- Reward: A numerical value reflecting the success of the chosen action (e.g., user satisfaction, accuracy of the generated response).
- Policy: The strategy used by the agent to select actions based on states.

Example: A Simplified RL Decision Engine Using Q-Learning
Below is a Python pseudocode example that illustrates how a basic Q-learning algorithm might be integrated into the decision engine.

python
Copy code

```python
import numpy as np

class RLDecisionEngine:
    def __init__(self, actions, learning_rate=0.1, discount_factor=0.9,
epsilon=0.2):
        self.actions = actions  # List of possible actions
        self.lr = learning_rate
        self.gamma = discount_factor
        self.epsilon = epsilon  # Exploration rate
        # Initialize Q-table with zeros: rows = states, columns = actions
        self.q_table = {}  # Using a dictionary for state-action pairs

    def get_q_values(self, state):
        # Return Q-values for the state, initialize if state not seen before
        if state not in self.q_table:
            self.q_table[state] = np.zeros(len(self.actions))
```

```python
        return self.q_table[state]

    def choose_action(self, state):
        q_values = self.get_q_values(state)
        # Epsilon-greedy action selection
        if np.random.rand() < self.epsilon:
            return np.random.choice(self.actions)
        else:
            return self.actions[np.argmax(q_values)]

    def update_q_value(self, state, action, reward, next_state):
        q_values = self.get_q_values(state)
        next_q_values = self.get_q_values(next_state)
        action_index = self.actions.index(action)
        # Q-learning update rule
        q_values[action_index] = q_values[action_index] + self.lr * (
            reward + self.gamma * np.max(next_q_values) -
q_values[action_index]
        )
        self.q_table[state] = q_values

# Example usage:
actions = ["generate_detailed_response", "request_more_information"]
rl_engine = RLDecisionEngine(actions)

# Define a simple state (e.g., "enough_docs" or "few_docs")
state = "enough_docs"
action = rl_engine.choose_action(state)
print("RL Chosen Action:", action)

# Simulate receiving a reward and moving to a new state
reward = 1.0  # Example reward
next_state = "enough_docs"
rl_engine.update_q_value(state, action, reward, next_state)
print("Updated Q-Table:", rl_engine.q_table)
```

Explanation:
- The RLDecisionEngine class uses a simple Q-learning algorithm to update its decision policy.
- The choose_action method implements an epsilon-greedy strategy to balance exploration and exploitation.

- The update_q_value method applies the Q-learning update rule based on received rewards.

9.3 Real-Time Decision Making and Adaptive Policies

Overview

Real-time decision making is crucial for systems that need to adapt on the fly to changes in the environment or user behavior. In such cases, the decision engine must process incoming data rapidly and adjust its policies as needed.

Strategies for Real-Time Decision Making

- Asynchronous Processing:
  Use asynchronous programming to handle multiple data streams concurrently, reducing latency.
- Adaptive Policies:
  Continuously update decision policies based on recent feedback. This might involve online learning techniques that adjust parameters without full retraining.
- Event-Driven Architecture:
  Design the system to trigger decision-making events as soon as new data becomes available.

Example: Asynchronous Decision Making with Python

Below is a simplified example using Python's asyncio library to simulate real-time decision-making.

python

Copy code

```python
import asyncio

async def process_decision(engine, state, delay=1):
    """
    Simulate processing a decision in real time.
    """
    await asyncio.sleep(delay)  # Simulate processing delay
    action = engine.choose_action(state)
    print(f"Processed action for state '{state}': {action}")
    return action

async def main():
    # Create an RL decision engine instance
    actions = ["generate_detailed_response", "request_more_information"]
    rl_engine = RLDecisionEngine(actions)
```

```
# Simulate real-time decision processing for multiple states
states = ["few_docs", "enough_docs", "few_docs"]
tasks = [process_decision(rl_engine, state, delay=i) for i, state in
enumerate(states, start=1)]

# Wait for all decisions to be processed
results = await asyncio.gather(*tasks)
print("Real-Time Decisions:", results)

# Run the asynchronous main function
asyncio.run(main())
```

Explanation:
- The process_decision function simulates a decision-making process with a delay.
- The main function creates multiple asynchronous tasks to process decisions concurrently.
- This example demonstrates how an asynchronous, real-time decision-making system can be implemented in Python.

9.4 Hybrid Models: Blending Rule-Based Systems with Learning Algorithms

Overview
Hybrid decision engines combine the reliability of rule-based systems with the adaptability of learning-based approaches. This blending leverages the strengths of both paradigms:
- Rule-Based Component: Provides a deterministic, interpretable baseline.
- Learning-Based Component: Adjusts policies dynamically based on data and feedback.

Advantages of Hybrid Models
- Robustness:
  The rule-based part ensures that critical decisions are made reliably.
- Flexibility:
  The learning component can adapt to new scenarios and improve performance over time.
- Transparency:
  Rules can be inspected and understood, while learning algorithms provide adaptive enhancements.

Comparative Table: Pure Rule-Based vs. Hybrid Decision Engines

Aspect	Pure Rule-Based	Hybrid Model
Determinism	Fully deterministic	Deterministic rules with adaptive adjustments
Adaptability	Limited flexibility	High adaptability through learning-based updates
Transparency	Highly interpretable	Transparent rules combined with less interpretable learned policies
Implementation	Simple, quick to deploy	More complex but offers long-term performance benefits

Example: A Hybrid Decision Engine

Below is a Python example that combines rule-based logic with a learning-based adjustment (using a simple threshold that can be modified by feedback).

python

Copy code

```
class HybridDecisionEngine:
    def __init__(self, rule_threshold=3, learning_engine=None):
        # Rule-based threshold for number of retrieved documents
        self.rule_threshold = rule_threshold
        # A learning-based component, e.g., an RLDecisionEngine instance
        self.learning_engine = learning_engine or RLDecisionEngine(
            actions=["generate_detailed_response",
"request_more_information"]
        )

    def decide(self, retrieved_docs, state):
        """
        Hybrid decision: First apply rule-based logic; then adjust using the
learning component.
        """
        # Rule-based decision
        if len(retrieved_docs) >= self.rule_threshold:
            rule_decision = "generate_detailed_response"
        else:
            rule_decision = "request_more_information"
```

```
    # Incorporate learning-based decision
    learning_decision = self.learning_engine.choose_action(state)

    # For demonstration, if both decisions agree, use that; otherwise,
prioritize rule-based
    if rule_decision == learning_decision:
        final_decision = rule_decision
    else:
        final_decision = rule_decision  # Prioritize rule-based decision for
safety

    return final_decision

# Example usage:
retrieved_docs_example = ["doc1", "doc2"]
state = "few_docs"
hybrid_engine = HybridDecisionEngine(rule_threshold=3)
decision = hybrid_engine.decide(retrieved_docs_example, state)
print("Hybrid Engine Decision:", decision)
```

Explanation:
- The HybridDecisionEngine class first applies a simple rule-based check on the number of retrieved documents.
- It then calls the learning-based component (an instance of RLDecisionEngine) to obtain an alternative decision based on the current state.
- Finally, it combines the two decisions—here, prioritizing the rule-based decision for safety. This approach can be refined to weight each component based on historical performance or confidence scores.

Summary
In Chapter 9, we explored the integration of autonomous decision-making into Agentic RAG systems:
- Designing the Decision Engine: We reviewed the key responsibilities and design considerations, and provided a simple rule-based engine example.
- Incorporating Reinforcement Learning: We introduced an RL-based decision engine using Q-learning, illustrating how policies can be updated from feedback.
- Real-Time Decision Making: We demonstrated asynchronous processing with Python's asyncio to enable adaptive, real-time decisions.

- Hybrid Models: We discussed the advantages of blending rule-based and learning-based approaches, and provided a hybrid engine example that leverages both methods.

By integrating these approaches, you can build a robust, adaptive decision engine that enhances the overall performance and responsiveness of your Agentic RAG system.

Chapter 10: End-to-End System Integration and Optimization

An Agentic RAG system brings together several distinct components—retrieval, generation, and decision-making—into a single pipeline that must operate efficiently and reliably. In this chapter, we focus on integrating these modules into an end-to-end system, optimizing its performance, deploying it in distributed and cloud environments, and establishing practices for ongoing monitoring and improvement.

10.1 Seamless Integration of Retrieval, Generation, and Decision Modules

Overview

For an Agentic RAG system to function effectively, the individual modules must work together seamlessly. This requires clear interfaces and well-defined data flows between:

- Retrieval Module: Responsible for fetching relevant documents or data.
- Generative Module: Produces text output by incorporating the retrieved context.
- Decision Engine: Determines the appropriate action (e.g., whether to generate a detailed response or ask for clarification) based on the input and retrieved information.

Integration Strategy

1. Standardized Data Formats:
   Define common data structures (e.g., JSON objects, Python dictionaries) that all modules use to exchange information.
2. Modular APIs:
   Each component should expose a simple API (or function interface) that other modules can call. This minimizes dependencies and simplifies testing.
3. Sequential Pipeline:
   The system should process a query in a sequential manner:
   - Step 1: The retrieval module processes the query and returns a list of relevant documents.
   - Step 2: The decision engine evaluates the retrieved data and determines the next step.
   - Step 3: The generative module uses both the query and the retrieved data (if appropriate) to generate the final response.

Example: End-to-End Integration Pipeline

Below is a simplified Python example that illustrates how to integrate the three modules into a cohesive pipeline.

python

Copy code

```python
# Define the individual modules (simplified versions)
class RetrievalModule:
    def __init__(self, corpus):
        self.corpus = corpus

    def retrieve(self, query):
        # Basic keyword matching (for demonstration)
        return [doc for doc in self.corpus if any(word.lower() in doc.lower() for
word in query.split())]

class GenerativeModule:
    def generate(self, query, context):
        # For simplicity, concatenate query and context; real-world use would
involve a language model.
        combined_context = " ".join(context)
        return f"Response to '{query}' with context: {combined_context}"

class DecisionEngine:
    def __init__(self, threshold=3):
        self.threshold = threshold

    def decide(self, retrieved_docs):
        if len(retrieved_docs) >= self.threshold:
            return "generate_detailed_response"
        else:
            return "request_more_information"

# Integration class for the Agentic RAG system
class AgenticRAGSystem:
    def __init__(self, corpus):
        self.retrieval_module = RetrievalModule(corpus)
        self.generative_module = GenerativeModule()
        self.decision_engine = DecisionEngine()

    def process_query(self, query):
        # Step 1: Retrieve relevant documents
        retrieved_docs = self.retrieval_module.retrieve(query)
        print("Retrieved Documents:", retrieved_docs)

        # Step 2: Decision engine determines the course of action
        decision = self.decision_engine.decide(retrieved_docs)
```

```python
        print("Decision:", decision)

        # Step 3: Generate response based on decision
        if decision == "generate_detailed_response":
            response = self.generative_module.generate(query, retrieved_docs)
        else:
            response = "Could you please provide more details?"
        return response

# Example usage:
corpus = [
    "Agentic RAG systems integrate retrieval and generation.",
    "Retrieval modules provide essential context.",
    "Decision engines guide the generation process.",
    "Modular architectures allow for flexible integration."
]
agentic_rag_system = AgenticRAGSystem(corpus)
query = "Explain the role of retrieval modules in AI."
final_response = no
agentic_rag_system.process_query(query)
print("Final Response:\n", final_response)
```

Explanation:
- RetrievalModule: Searches the corpus using basic keyword matching.
- DecisionEngine: Checks if the number of retrieved documents meets a threshold.
- GenerativeModule: Generates a simple response by combining the query with the retrieved context.
- AgenticRAGSystem: Integrates these modules into a single pipeline that processes a query step by step.

10.2 Optimizing System Performance and Resource Management

Performance Optimization Strategies
1. Caching:
   Cache frequently retrieved documents or intermediate results using in-memory data stores like Redis to reduce repeated computations.
2. Parallel Processing:
   Leverage multi-threading or multi-processing to handle simultaneous queries or to process independent modules concurrently.

3. Efficient Algorithms:
   Use approximate nearest neighbor (ANN) algorithms (e.g., FAISS) for faster vector-based retrieval, and optimize neural model inference with techniques like model quantization.
4. Load Balancing:
   Distribute incoming queries evenly across multiple instances of the system components using load balancers.

Resource Management

- Memory Optimization:
  Use data structures and algorithms that minimize memory overhead, and offload large datasets to disk-based or distributed storage when possible.
- Compute Resource Allocation:
  Monitor CPU, GPU, and memory usage, and allocate resources dynamically based on demand. Cloud platforms often provide autoscaling features.

Comparative Table: Optimization Techniques

Aspect	Technique	Benefits
Speed	Caching, Parallel Processing	Reduces latency and improves throughput
Accuracy	Efficient Algorithms (ANN, quantization)	Maintains performance with lower compute costs
Resource Management	Load Balancing, Autoscaling	Dynamically allocates resources to meet demand

10.3 Distributed Architectures and Cloud Deployment Strategies

Distributed Architectures

Distributed architectures help scale the system to handle large volumes of data and high query rates. Key strategies include:

- Microservices Architecture:
  Decompose the system into independent services (e.g., separate services for retrieval, generation, and decision-making) that communicate via APIs.
- Containerization:
  Use Docker to package each module as a container. This simplifies deployment and scaling, ensuring consistency across environments.

- Orchestration:
  Tools like Kubernetes allow for automated deployment, scaling, and management of containerized applications.

Cloud Deployment Strategies

1. Cloud Providers:
   Deploy on cloud platforms such as AWS, Google Cloud, or Azure. These providers offer managed services for compute, storage, and networking.
2. Serverless Architectures:
   Use serverless computing (e.g., AWS Lambda) for components with variable loads, reducing infrastructure management overhead.
3. Hybrid Deployments:
   Combine on-premises infrastructure with cloud resources for sensitive data processing and scalability.

Example: Docker Compose for Microservices Integration

Below is a simplified docker-compose.yml file example that demonstrates how to deploy a microservices-based Agentic RAG system with separate containers for each module.

yaml

Copy code

```yaml
version: '3'
services:
 retrieval:
  image: myorg/retrieval-module:latest
  ports:
   - "5001:5001"
 generation:
  image: myorg/generative-module:latest
  ports:
   - "5002:5002"
 decision:
  image: myorg/decision-engine:latest
  ports:
   - "5003:5003"
 agentic_rag:
  image: myorg/agentic-rag-system:latest
  ports:
   - "5000:5000"
  depends_on:
   - retrieval
   - generation
   - decision
```

Explanation:
- Each module is deployed as a separate container.
- The agentic_rag service depends on the retrieval, generation, and decision services.
- This configuration allows for independent scaling and management of each module.

10.4 Monitoring, Debugging, and Continuous Improvement Practices

Monitoring
Effective monitoring ensures that the system operates reliably and helps detect issues early. Key practices include:
- Logging:
  Implement structured logging for each module to capture errors, performance metrics, and user interactions.
- Monitoring Tools:
  Use tools like Prometheus for metrics collection and Grafana for visualization. Cloud providers also offer integrated monitoring services (e.g., AWS CloudWatch).
- Alerting:
  Set up alerts to notify the operations team when performance metrics deviate from expected ranges or when errors occur.

Debugging
To efficiently diagnose and fix issues:
- Centralized Logging:
  Aggregate logs from all modules using tools like the ELK Stack (Elasticsearch, Logstash, Kibana) to facilitate search and analysis.
- Tracing:
  Implement distributed tracing (e.g., using Jaeger or Zipkin) to follow the flow of requests through the system, which is especially valuable in microservices architectures.

Continuous Improvement
Continuous improvement involves regularly updating and refining the system based on performance data and user feedback:
- A/B Testing:
  Deploy different versions of the system (or individual modules) to compare performance and select the best performing variant.

- Feedback Loops:
  Incorporate user feedback and performance metrics to adjust algorithms, update models, and refine policies.
- Automated Deployment:
  Use continuous integration/continuous deployment (CI/CD) pipelines to ensure that updates are tested and deployed rapidly and reliably.

Example: Simple Monitoring with Python Logging

Below is a Python code snippet that demonstrates how to set up basic logging for system events.

python
Copy code

```python
import logging

# Configure logging
logging.basicConfig(
    level=logging.INFO,
    format='%(asctime)s [%(levelname)s] %(message)s',
    handlers=[
        logging.FileHandler("agentic_rag_system.log"),
        logging.StreamHandler()
    ]
)

def log_event(event_message, level="info"):
    if level == "info":
        logging.info(event_message)
    elif level == "error":
        logging.error(event_message)
    else:
        logging.debug(event_message)

# Example usage:
log_event("Agentic RAG system started successfully.")
log_event("Retrieval module returned 5 documents for query 'autonomous systems'.")
log_event("Error: Generation module encountered a timeout.",
level="error")
```

Explanation:
- logging.basicConfig: Configures logging to output messages to both a file and the console.

- log_event: A helper function to log events at different severity levels.
- This simple setup aids in monitoring system behavior and debugging issues.

Summary

In Chapter 10, we examined the integration and optimization of an end-to-end Agentic RAG system:

- Seamless Integration:
  We detailed the integration of retrieval, generation, and decision modules into a unified pipeline, complete with an end-to-end code example.
- Performance and Resource Optimization:
  Techniques such as caching, parallel processing, and efficient algorithms were discussed alongside a comparative table of optimization strategies.
- Distributed Architectures and Cloud Deployment:
  We reviewed microservices, containerization, orchestration, and provided an example using Docker Compose for deploying the system.
- Monitoring, Debugging, and Continuous Improvement:
  We highlighted logging, monitoring tools, distributed tracing, and practices for continuous updates, supported by sample code for logging.

By applying these strategies and practices, you can build a robust, scalable, and efficient Agentic RAG system that is well-equipped to meet real-time demands while continuously improving over time.

Chapter 11: Implementation Strategies and Best Practices

A successful Agentic RAG system not only requires strong theoretical foundations but also demands robust implementation practices. This chapter covers the tools and frameworks you can use, provides detailed tutorials and code walkthroughs, and describes best practices in software engineering, deployment, and system maintenance.

11.1 Overview of Frameworks, Libraries, and Tools

When implementing an Agentic RAG system, leveraging established frameworks and libraries can significantly accelerate development and ensure high quality. Below is an overview of some of the key tools:

Popular Frameworks and Libraries

Tool/Library	Purpose	Key Features	Common Use Cases
PyTorch	Deep learning framework	Dynamic computation graphs, strong community support	Model development, prototyping, research
TensorFlow	Deep learning framework	Scalable deployment, production-ready, TensorFlow Serving	Large-scale model training and deployment
Hugging Face Transformers	Pretrained language models and NLP pipelines	Easy-to-use API for transformers (e.g., GPT, BERT, T5)	Fine-tuning, text generation, NLP tasks
FAISS	Approximate nearest neighbor search library	Efficient high-dimensional vector search	Dense vector retrieval in large corpora
Elasticsearch	Search and analytics engine	Distributed search, RESTful API,	Text retrieval and search

		real-time indexing	engine integration
Docker	Containerizati on platform	Isolated environments, reproducibility, portability	Packaging and deployment of microservices
Kubernetes	Container orchestration system	Automated deployment, scaling, and management of containers	Managing distributed AI services
Redis	In-memory data store and cache	Fast read/write performance, data structures support	Caching query results, session management
Prometheus & Grafana	Monitoring and visualization tools	Metrics collection, alerting, customizable dashboards	Real-time monitoring and system performance tracking

Key Considerations

- Framework Compatibility: Choose frameworks that integrate well with your overall technology stack.
- Scalability and Performance: For production environments, select tools that can scale (e.g., TensorFlow for production model serving, Kubernetes for orchestrating microservices).
- Ease of Use and Community Support: Libraries like Hugging Face Transformers have extensive documentation and active communities that can be invaluable during development.

11.2 Step-by-Step Implementation Tutorials and Code Walkthroughs

In this section, we outline a step-by-step guide for implementing key components of the Agentic RAG system with detailed code examples.

Example: Building a Simple Agentic RAG Pipeline

Let's walk through a simplified pipeline that integrates the retrieval, generation, and decision modules.

Step 1: Define the Retrieval Module

python

Copy code

```python
class RetrievalModule:
    def __init__(self, corpus):
        self.corpus = corpus

    def retrieve(self, query):
        # Perform simple keyword matching for demonstration
        return [doc for doc in self.corpus if any(word.lower() in doc.lower() for word in query.split())]

# Example corpus
corpus = [
    "Agentic RAG systems integrate retrieval and generation.",
    "Retrieval modules provide essential context.",
    "Decision engines guide the generation process.",
    "Modular architectures allow for flexible integration."
]
```

Step 2: Define the Generative Module
python
Copy code

```python
class GenerativeModule:
    def generate(self, query, context):
        # In practice, integrate a transformer model. Here, we simulate generation.
        combined_context = " ".join(context)
        return f"Response to '{query}': {combined_context}"

# Simple demonstration using string concatenation
```

Step 3: Define the Decision Engine
python
Copy code

```python
class DecisionEngine:
    def __init__(self, threshold=3):
        self.threshold = threshold

    def decide(self, retrieved_docs):
        if len(retrieved_docs) >= self.threshold:
            return "generate_detailed_response"
        else:
```

```python
        return "request_more_information"
```

Step 4: Integrate into an End-to-End Pipeline
python
Copy code
```python
class AgenticRAGSystem:
    def __init__(self, corpus):
        self.retrieval_module = RetrievalModule(corpus)
        self.generative_module = GenerativeModule()
        self.decision_engine = DecisionEngine()

    def process_query(self, query):
        # Retrieve relevant documents
        retrieved_docs = self.retrieval_module.retrieve(query)
        print("Retrieved Documents:", retrieved_docs)

        # Decision-making process
        decision = self.decision_engine.decide(retrieved_docs)
        print("Decision:", decision)

        # Generate final response based on decision
        if decision == "generate_detailed_response":
            return self.generative_module.generate(query, retrieved_docs)
        else:
            return "Could you please provide more details?"

# Run the integrated system
agentic_rag_system = AgenticRAGSystem(corpus)
query = "Explain the role of retrieval in AI systems."
response = agentic_rag_system.process_query(query)
print("Final Response:\n", response)
```

Walkthrough Explanation:
- Retrieval Module: Searches the corpus using a simple keyword match.
- Decision Engine: Evaluates if the number of retrieved documents meets the threshold.
- Generative Module: Simulates response generation by combining the query and retrieved context.
- Integration: The AgenticRAGSystem class ties all components together to process a query end-to-end.

11.3 Software Engineering Practices for Reliable AI Systems

Building reliable AI systems requires strong software engineering practices that ensure code quality, scalability, and maintainability.

Best Practices

1. Version Control:
   Use Git to manage code changes, collaborate with team members, and maintain a history of your project.
2. Modular Code Structure:
   Organize code into modules and packages (as demonstrated in previous examples) to isolate functionality and simplify testing.
3. Automated Testing:
   Implement unit tests and integration tests using frameworks like pytest to catch bugs early and ensure that changes do not break existing functionality.
4. Continuous Integration/Continuous Deployment (CI/CD):
   Use CI/CD tools (e.g., GitHub Actions, Jenkins) to automate testing and deployment, ensuring that new changes are deployed smoothly and reliably.
5. Documentation:
   Maintain clear documentation for your codebase, including inline comments, README files, and API documentation.
6. Logging and Monitoring:
   Implement logging (using Python's logging module) and integrate monitoring solutions to track system performance and quickly identify issues.

Example: Basic Unit Testing with pytest

Below is an example of a simple unit test for the retrieval module.

python

Copy code

```python
# test_retrieval.py
import pytest
from retrieval_module import RetrievalModule

def test_retrieve():
    corpus = [
        "Agentic RAG systems integrate retrieval and generation.",
        "Retrieval modules provide essential context.",
        "Decision engines guide the generation process."
    ]
    module = RetrievalModule(corpus)
    query = "retrieval"
    results = module.retrieve(query)
    # Check that at least one document is retrieved
```

```
    assert len(results) > 0
    # Check that the word "retrieval" appears in the results
    for doc in results:
        assert "retrieval" in doc.lower()

if __name__ == "__main__":
    pytest.main()
```

Explanation:
- pytest: A popular testing framework for Python.
- test_retrieve: Defines a test case that ensures the retrieval module returns documents containing the keyword "retrieval."
- Running pytest will execute the test and report any failures.

11.4 Deployment, Maintenance, and Upgrades

Deployment Strategies
1. Containerization:
   Use Docker to package each component of your system into containers, ensuring consistency across development and production environments.
2. Orchestration:
   Deploy containers using Kubernetes or Docker Compose to manage scaling, load balancing, and rolling updates.
3. Cloud Deployment:
   Utilize cloud platforms (AWS, Google Cloud, Azure) for scalable infrastructure. Many providers offer managed services for containers, databases, and monitoring.

Maintenance and Upgrades
- Continuous Monitoring:
  Implement monitoring (using Prometheus, Grafana, or cloud-native solutions) to keep track of system health, performance, and errors.
- Regular Updates:
  Schedule periodic updates for your models, libraries, and system components to incorporate improvements, security patches, and new features.
- Rollback Mechanisms:
  Ensure that your deployment strategy supports quick rollbacks in case an upgrade introduces issues.
- Documentation and Changelogs:
  Maintain detailed documentation and changelogs to track changes over time and facilitate troubleshooting.

Example: Docker Compose Deployment Configuration

Below is a sample docker-compose.yml file for deploying a microservices-based Agentic RAG system:

yaml

Copy code

```yaml
version: '3'
services:
  retrieval:
    image: myorg/retrieval-module:latest
    ports:
      - "5001:5001"
  generation:
    image: myorg/generative-module:latest
    ports:
      - "5002:5002"
  decision:
    image: myorg/decision-engine:latest
    ports:
      - "5003:5003"
  agentic_rag:
    image: myorg/agentic-rag-system:latest
    ports:
      - "5000:5000"
    depends_on:
      - retrieval
      - generation
      - decision
```

Explanation:
- Services: Defines separate containers for retrieval, generation, and decision modules.
- Ports: Maps container ports to host ports.
- depends_on: Ensures the main system waits for the dependent modules to be up and running.
- This configuration facilitates easy scaling and management of each component.

Summary

In Chapter 11, we explored implementation strategies and best practices essential for building and maintaining a robust Agentic RAG system:
- Overview of Frameworks, Libraries, and Tools:
  We reviewed popular tools like PyTorch, TensorFlow, Hugging Face

Transformers, Docker, Kubernetes, and more, emphasizing their roles in system development.

- Step-by-Step Implementation Tutorials and Code Walkthroughs:
  We provided a detailed walkthrough of integrating retrieval, generation, and decision modules into a cohesive pipeline with clear code examples.
- Software Engineering Practices:
  Best practices including version control, modular code, automated testing, CI/CD, logging, and documentation were discussed to ensure system reliability.
- Deployment, Maintenance, and Upgrades:
  Strategies for containerization, cloud deployment, continuous monitoring, and maintenance were detailed, along with an example Docker Compose configuration.

By following these strategies and best practices, you will be well-equipped to implement, deploy, and maintain a high-quality, scalable Agentic RAG system that can evolve with emerging requirements and technological advances.

Chapter 12: Case Studies and Real-World Applications

Agentic Retrieval-Augmented Generation (RAG) systems have far-reaching potential across industries due to their ability to retrieve relevant, up-to-date information and generate context-aware responses while autonomously adapting to new situations. In this chapter, we explore case studies and applications in several key domains:

- Healthcare: Diagnostics, decision support, and beyond
- Financial Services: Risk management and automated customer support
- Customer Interaction: Enhancing engagement with chatbots and virtual assistants
- Emerging Domains: Robotics, IoT, and autonomous vehicles

Each section provides an overview of the challenges, describes the implementation of Agentic RAG components in the domain, and outlines the benefits achieved.

12.1 Healthcare: Diagnostics, Decision Support, and Beyond

Overview

In the healthcare domain, timely and accurate information is critical for diagnostics and decision support. Agentic RAG systems can assist medical professionals by:

- Retrieving Up-to-Date Medical Literature: Accessing recent research, clinical guidelines, and patient records.
- Generating Diagnostic Recommendations: Integrating retrieved information with patient data to produce potential diagnoses and treatment options.
- Supporting Decision-Making: Offering decision support by summarizing relevant evidence, suggesting next steps, and highlighting risks.

Real-World Application Example

Case Study: Diagnostic Support System

A hospital deploys an Agentic RAG system to support physicians in diagnosing complex cases. The system integrates:

- Retrieval Module: Searches an extensive database of clinical studies, case reports, and drug information.
- Generative Module: Uses a fine-tuned transformer model to generate a concise summary of the retrieved literature, highlighting key findings.
- Decision Engine: Evaluates the relevance of retrieved documents and determines whether the system should suggest a complete diagnostic hypothesis or ask for further clinical details.

Benefits

- Improved Diagnostic Accuracy: By grounding suggestions in the latest medical research.

- Reduced Cognitive Load: Physicians receive summarized insights rather than sifting through voluminous literature.
- Faster Decision-Making: Real-time retrieval and generation help in emergencies or high-pressure environments.

Illustrative Table: Healthcare Application Overview

Component	Function	Healthcare-Specific Considerations
Retrieval Module	Fetch clinical studies, patient histories, guidelines	Must access HIPAA-compliant, up-to-date medical databases
Generative Module	Summarize and generate diagnostic insights	Needs fine-tuning on medical corpora and terminology
Decision Engine	Determine whether to output a diagnostic summary or request additional patient data	Must balance comprehensiveness with clarity for clinical use

Pseudocode Example: Diagnostic Recommendation
python

Copy code

```
# Pseudocode for a diagnostic support function
def diagnostic_support(patient_symptoms, patient_history,
medical_corpus):
    # Step 1: Retrieve relevant documents
    retrieved_docs = retrieval_module.retrieve(query=patient_symptoms + "
" + patient_history)

    # Step 2: Decision engine assesses whether enough data has been
retrieved
    decision = decision_engine.decide(retrieved_docs)

    # Step 3: Generate diagnostic recommendation or request more info
    if decision == "generate_detailed_response":
        recommendation =
generative_module.generate(query=patient_symptoms,
context=retrieved_docs)
    else:
```

```
    recommendation = "Additional clinical details are required."

    return recommendation

# Example usage:
symptoms = "chest pain, shortness of breath"
history = "history of hypertension"
recommendation = diagnostic_support(symptoms, history,
medical_corpus)
print("Diagnostic Recommendation:", recommendation)
```

Explanation:
- The pseudocode outlines how the system integrates patient data with medical literature retrieval and decision-making to generate a diagnostic recommendation.

12.2 Financial Services: Risk Management and Automated Customer Support

Overview

In financial services, the ability to rapidly process vast amounts of data and generate accurate, context-specific insights is critical for risk management and customer support.

Agentic RAG systems in this domain can:
- Monitor Market Data and News: Retrieve relevant financial news, market trends, and regulatory updates.
- Automate Customer Support: Provide real-time responses to customer queries related to accounts, investments, and risk management.
- Enhance Decision-Making: Offer risk assessments, fraud detection, and investment advice based on both historical data and real-time information.

Real-World Application Example

Case Study: Automated Risk Assessment and Customer Support

A financial institution implements an Agentic RAG system to enhance its risk management and customer service operations. The system components include:
- Retrieval Module: Searches real-time financial news, regulatory filings, and internal risk reports.
- Generative Module: Produces risk assessment summaries or answers customer queries.
- Decision Engine: Determines whether to flag potential risks, initiate fraud alerts, or route customer queries to human agents for complex issues.

Benefits

- Proactive Risk Management: Early identification of market risks and fraudulent activities.
- Enhanced Customer Experience: Automated, accurate, and timely responses improve customer satisfaction.
- Operational Efficiency: Reduces the need for manual data analysis and supports compliance with regulatory requirements.

Illustrative Table: Financial Services Application Overview

Component	Function	Financial-Specific Considerations
Retrieval Module	Fetch market data, news articles, risk reports	Must handle high-frequency data and ensure real-time updates
Generative Module	Generate risk assessments and support responses	Requires fine-tuning on financial jargon and regulatory language
Decision Engine	Decide on risk alerts, fraud detection, or query escalation	Needs to incorporate thresholds and regulatory compliance checks

Pseudocode Example: Risk Assessment

python

Copy code

```python
def risk_assessment(customer_query, financial_corpus):
    # Retrieve market data and relevant financial documents
    retrieved_docs = retrieval_module.retrieve(query=customer_query)

    # Decision engine evaluates whether enough evidence exists for a risk alert
    decision = decision_engine.decide(retrieved_docs)

    if decision == "generate_detailed_response":
        assessment = generative_module.generate(query=customer_query, context=retrieved_docs)
    else:
        assessment = "Please provide additional financial details."

    return assessment

# Example usage:
```

```
query = "High volatility in tech stocks"
assessment_result = risk_assessment(query, financial_corpus)
print("Risk Assessment Result:", assessment_result)
```

Explanation:

- This pseudocode demonstrates how the system retrieves financial documents, uses the decision engine to evaluate the information, and generates a risk assessment summary.

12.3 Enhancing Customer Interaction with Chatbots and Virtual Assistants

Overview

Chatbots and virtual assistants are increasingly used in customer service to provide quick, accurate, and personalized support. Agentic RAG systems empower these interfaces by:

- Retrieving Contextual Information: Accessing product databases, FAQs, and user histories.
- Generating Conversational Responses: Producing natural language responses that address customer queries effectively.
- Autonomous Adaptation: Learning from interactions to improve future responses and overall engagement.

Real-World Application Example

Case Study: Customer Service Chatbot

A retail company deploys a chatbot powered by an Agentic RAG system. The system:

- Retrieval Module: Searches internal knowledge bases, past customer interactions, and product catalogs.
- Generative Module: Crafts personalized responses that combine customer-specific data with general product information.
- Decision Engine: Determines whether to provide an automated response or escalate the query to a human representative if the query is too complex.

Benefits

- Improved Response Times: Automated responses reduce customer wait times.
- Personalized Interaction: The system tailors responses based on customer data and previous interactions.
- Cost Reduction: Reduces the need for a large customer service team while maintaining high service quality.

Illustrative Table: Chatbot Application Overview

Component	Function	Customer Service Considerations

Retrieval Module	Fetch product details, FAQs, and customer history	Must access up-to-date, structured product and customer data
Generative Module	Generate natural, personalized responses	Needs to maintain conversational tone and clarity
Decision Engine	Decide on automated response or human escalation	Critical for handling complex or sensitive customer issues

Example: Chatbot Interaction Code Snippet

python

Copy code

```python
def chatbot_response(user_query, customer_profile):
    # Combine the user query with customer-specific details
    augmented_query = user_query + " " + customer_profile.get('preferences', '')
    # Retrieve relevant documents (e.g., product info, FAQs)
    retrieved_docs = retrieval_module.retrieve(augmented_query)
    # Decision engine determines whether to respond automatically
    decision = decision_engine.decide(retrieved_docs)

    if decision == "generate_detailed_response":
        response = generative_module.generate(query=user_query, context=retrieved_docs)
    else:
        response = "Let me connect you with a human agent for further assistance."
    return response

# Example usage:
customer_profile = {"preferences": "interested in eco-friendly products"}
user_query = "What are the sustainable options for home appliances?"
chatbot_reply = chatbot_response(user_query, customer_profile)
print("Chatbot Reply:\n", chatbot_reply)
```

Explanation:

- This example demonstrates how a chatbot uses the retrieval, decision, and generative modules to provide a personalized response based on a customer query and profile.

12.4 Emerging Domains: Robotics, IoT, and Autonomous Vehicles

Overview

Agentic RAG systems are also finding applications in emerging domains where real-time decision making and context awareness are critical:

- Robotics:
  Robots can use RAG systems to retrieve environmental data, generate plans, and adapt autonomously to dynamic situations.
- Internet of Things (IoT):
  IoT devices benefit from RAG systems by integrating sensor data with external information (e.g., weather forecasts) to optimize operations.
- Autonomous Vehicles:
  Self-driving cars use similar architectures to retrieve map data, traffic information, and sensor readings to make immediate, context-aware driving decisions.

Real-World Application Example

Case Study: Autonomous Vehicle Navigation

An autonomous vehicle is equipped with an Agentic RAG system to enhance its navigation capabilities:

- Retrieval Module: Retrieves real-time traffic updates, road conditions, and navigation maps.
- Generative Module: Processes the retrieved data to generate optimal route recommendations and driving instructions.
- Decision Engine: Determines whether to continue on the current route, adjust speed, or take an alternate route based on dynamic environmental inputs.

Benefits

- Enhanced Safety: Real-time adaptation to road conditions and traffic ensures safer navigation.
- Efficiency: Optimizes routes to reduce travel time and fuel consumption.
- Scalability: The system can be deployed across fleets of vehicles, continuously learning and improving.

Illustrative Table: Autonomous Vehicle Application Overview

Component	Function	Domain-Specific Considerations

Retrieval Module	Fetch traffic, weather, and map data	Must process data from multiple sensors and external sources
Generative Module	Generate driving instructions and route plans	Requires high precision and real-time processing
Decision Engine	Adaptively select the optimal navigation strategy	Critical for safety and operational efficiency in dynamic environments

Pseudocode Example: Autonomous Navigation Decision

python

Copy code

```python
def autonomous_navigation(sensor_data, external_data):
    # Merge sensor data (e.g., from cameras, LIDAR) with external sources (traffic, weather)
    combined_query = sensor_data + " " + external_data
    # Retrieve contextual information (e.g., map data, traffic reports)
    retrieved_docs = retrieval_module.retrieve(combined_query)
    # Decision engine determines navigation action based on the current context
    decision = decision_engine.decide(retrieved_docs)

    if decision == "generate_detailed_response":
        route_plan = generative_module.generate(query=combined_query, context=retrieved_docs)
    else:
        route_plan = "Alert: Adjust driving strategy; additional sensor calibration required."

    return route_plan

# Example usage:
sensor_data = "Obstacle detected at 200m ahead"
external_data = "Heavy traffic on main road, light rain"
navigation_plan = autonomous_navigation(sensor_data, external_data)
print("Navigation Plan:\n", navigation_plan)
```

Explanation:
- The pseudocode simulates how an autonomous vehicle might combine sensor data with external data, use the retrieval module to fetch relevant information, and apply the decision engine and generative module to produce a navigation plan.

Summary

In Chapter 12, we explored several case studies and real-world applications of Agentic RAG systems:
- Healthcare:
  Demonstrated how diagnostic support systems integrate retrieval, generation, and decision-making to provide timely, evidence-based recommendations.
- Financial Services:
  Illustrated applications in risk management and automated customer support, enhancing decision-making with real-time financial data.
- Customer Interaction:
  Showed how chatbots and virtual assistants use Agentic RAG to deliver personalized and efficient customer service.
- Emerging Domains:
  Explored the role of RAG systems in robotics, IoT, and autonomous vehicles, highlighting real-time decision-making and adaptive navigation.

Through detailed explanations, comparative tables, and illustrative code examples, this chapter demonstrates the versatility and practical impact of Agentic RAG systems across a range of industries. These real-world applications underscore the potential of integrating retrieval-augmented generation with autonomous decision-making to create innovative, high-performance solutions.

Chapter 13: Experimental Design and Benchmarking

A rigorous experimental design and benchmarking process is crucial for evaluating the performance of Agentic RAG systems. In this chapter, we cover four major areas:

1. Designing Experiments for Agentic RAG Systems: How to set up experiments to test the effectiveness of the integrated retrieval, generation, and decision-making components.
2. Evaluation Metrics and Performance Indicators: The criteria used to assess the quality and efficiency of the system.
3. Benchmarking Against Traditional and Cutting-Edge Models: Strategies to compare Agentic RAG systems with baseline methods and state-of-the-art models.
4. Iterative Analysis and System Refinement: Techniques for continuously improving system performance based on experimental feedback.

13.1 Designing Experiments for Agentic RAG Systems

Goals and Considerations

When designing experiments for Agentic RAG systems, consider the following goals:

- Effectiveness: Determine how well the system retrieves relevant information, generates coherent responses, and makes autonomous decisions.
- Efficiency: Measure the latency and resource usage of the integrated system.
- Robustness: Evaluate how the system performs under varying conditions (e.g., different types of queries or noisy inputs).

Experimental Setup

1. Data Preparation:
   - Training and Test Splits: Ensure you have a representative split of data for training, validation, and testing.
   - Benchmark Datasets: Use domain-specific datasets (e.g., medical records for healthcare, financial news for risk management) to test performance in real-world scenarios.
2. Baseline Models:
   - Compare against traditional generative models (e.g., GPT variants without retrieval augmentation) and other hybrid systems.
   - Establish simple rule-based systems as additional baselines for decision-making components.
3. Controlled Variables:
   - Query Complexity: Vary the complexity of input queries to assess system adaptability.

- ○ Corpus Size: Experiment with different corpus sizes to evaluate scalability.
- ○ Response Length: Set limits on output length to study generation quality versus response conciseness.

Example: Experimental Design Pseudocode

python

Copy code

```python
def run_experiment(agentic_rag_system, test_queries, evaluation_metric):
    results = {}
    for query in test_queries:
        # Process the query through the integrated system
        response = agentic_rag_system.process_query(query)
        # Evaluate the response using a chosen metric (e.g., BLEU score, human rating)
        score = evaluation_metric(query, response)
        results[query] = {
            "response": response,
            "score": score
        }
    return results


# Example usage:
test_queries = [
    "Explain the role of retrieval in diagnostic support.",
    "What are the risk factors for volatile tech stocks?",
    "How do eco-friendly products impact home appliance choices?"
]


# A dummy evaluation metric for demonstration (in practice, replace with actual metric computation)
def dummy_metric(query, response):
    # Returns a random score for demonstration purposes
    import random
    return random.uniform(0, 1)


# Run experiment on a pre-configured Agentic RAG system
experiment_results = run_experiment(agentic_rag_system, test_queries, dummy_metric)
print("Experiment Results:")
for query, result in experiment_results.items():
```

```
print(f"Query: {query}\nScore: {result['score']:.2f}\nResponse:
{result['response']}\n")
```

Explanation:
- The pseudocode defines an experimental loop that processes a list of test queries through the Agentic RAG system.
- An evaluation metric function (here, a dummy function) computes a score for each response.
- Results are stored in a dictionary for later analysis.

13.2 Evaluation Metrics and Performance Indicators

Key Evaluation Metrics

Evaluating the performance of a generative system involves both automated and human-centered metrics. Common evaluation metrics include:

Metric	Description	Pros	Cons
BLEU	Measures n-gram overlap between generated text and reference text	Widely used in machine translation	May not capture semantic meaning accurately
ROUGE	Focuses on recall of n-grams, commonly used for summarization tasks	Effective for summarization quality	Can be insensitive to paraphrasing and style differences
Perplexity	Quantifies how well a probability model predicts a sample (lower is better)	Directly reflects model uncertainty	May not correlate with human judgments of quality
BERTScore	Uses contextual embeddings to compare semantic similarity between texts	Captures semantic similarity better	Computationally expensive

Human Evaluation	Subjective assessment by human judges on fluency, relevance, and coherence	Provides a comprehensive quality assessment	Time-consuming and subjective

Performance Indicators

In addition to quality metrics, consider these performance indicators:

- Latency: Time taken to process a query and generate a response.
- Throughput: Number of queries processed per unit time.
- Resource Utilization: CPU, GPU, and memory usage during inference.

Example: Calculating Perplexity (Revisited)

Below is an example using a pre-trained model to compute perplexity as a performance metric:

python

Copy code

```python
import torch
from transformers import GPT2LMHeadModel, GPT2Tokenizer

def calculate_perplexity(text, model, tokenizer):
    encodings = tokenizer(text, return_tensors='pt')
    max_length = model.config.n_positions
    stride = 512
    nlls = []
    for i in range(0, encodings.input_ids.size(1), stride):
        begin_loc = max(i + stride - max_length, 0)
        end_loc = i + stride
        input_ids = encodings.input_ids[:, begin_loc:end_loc]
        target_ids = input_ids.clone()
        target_ids[:, :-stride] = -100  # Mask tokens not to be predicted
        with torch.no_grad():
            outputs = model(input_ids, labels=target_ids)
            neg_log_likelihood = outputs.loss * stride
        nlls.append(neg_log_likelihood)
    ppl = torch.exp(torch.stack(nlls).sum() / end_loc)
    return ppl.item()

# Example usage:
model = GPT2LMHeadModel.from_pretrained('gpt2')
tokenizer = GPT2Tokenizer.from_pretrained('gpt2')
```

```
sample_text = "Agentic RAG systems combine retrieval with autonomous
decision making."
ppl_value = calculate_perplexity(sample_text, model, tokenizer)
print("Perplexity:", ppl_value)
```

Explanation:
- The function computes the negative log-likelihood (NLL) over chunks of the input text and calculates perplexity.
- Perplexity is a useful automated metric to gauge model performance, with lower values indicating better predictive performance.

13.3 Benchmarking Against Traditional and Cutting-Edge Models

Establishing Baselines

To assess the performance of an Agentic RAG system, it is essential to benchmark it against various baseline models:

1. Traditional Generative Models:
   Models that generate text based solely on pre-trained language models without retrieval augmentation.
2. Hybrid Systems:
   Systems that integrate retrieval with generation using simpler decision mechanisms.
3. State-of-the-Art Models:
   Recently developed models that may employ advanced techniques such as dense retrieval, Fusion-in-Decoder (FiD), or reinforcement learning enhancements.

Comparative Benchmarking Table

Model Type	Description	Expected Performance	Key Metrics
Traditional Generative Models	Models like vanilla GPT that generate based solely on internal data	Lower factual accuracy and context relevance	BLEU, Perplexity, Human Evaluation
Basic Hybrid RAG Systems	Integrates retrieval with a rule-based decision engine	Improved accuracy over pure generative models	ROUGE, BERTScore, Latency

Advanced Agentic RAG Systems	Uses autonomous decision-making, reinforcement learning, and advanced integration techniques	Highest context relevance, adaptability, and accuracy	Combined metrics (BLEU, ROUGE, Perplexity), Real-Time Performance

Benchmarking Methodology

- Controlled Experiments:
  Run the same set of queries across all models.
- Statistical Analysis:
  Compare average metric scores and perform significance testing (e.g., paired t-tests) to determine if differences are statistically significant.
- Human Evaluations:
  Complement automated metrics with human judgments to assess overall quality and usability.

13.4 Iterative Analysis and System Refinement

Iterative Process

Building an effective Agentic RAG system is an iterative process involving:

1. Data Collection and Preprocessing:
   Continuously update and refine the data pipelines based on error analysis and feedback.
2. Hyperparameter Tuning:
   Experiment with different model parameters (e.g., learning rates, threshold values in the decision engine) to improve performance.
3. Error Analysis:
   Regularly analyze system outputs to identify patterns of errors or weaknesses.
   - For instance, if the system frequently requests additional information on certain types of queries, this may indicate insufficient retrieval or suboptimal decision thresholds.
4. A/B Testing:
   Deploy multiple versions of the system in parallel and compare user interactions and feedback to determine which configuration performs best.

Example: Iterative Refinement Pseudocode

python

Copy code

```python
def iterative_refinement(agentic_rag_system, test_queries,
evaluation_metric, num_iterations=5):
```

```python
    best_config = None
    best_score = float('-inf')

    for iteration in range(num_iterations):
        print(f"Iteration {iteration+1} starting...")
        # Optionally adjust system parameters for this iteration
        # e.g., modify decision engine threshold or adjust sampling parameters
in the generative module

        # Run experiments on test queries
        results = run_experiment(agentic_rag_system, test_queries,
evaluation_metric)
        # Calculate average score across all queries
        avg_score = sum(result["score"] for result in results.values()) /
len(results)
        print(f"Iteration {iteration+1} average score: {avg_score:.2f}")

        # Check if current iteration outperforms previous best
        if avg_score > best_score:
            best_score = avg_score
            best_config = agentic_rag_system.get_config()  # Assume a method
to get current system configuration

        # Optionally incorporate feedback to refine system parameters here

    print("Best configuration found:", best_config)
    return best_config

# Example usage:
best_system_config = iterative_refinement(agentic_rag_system,
test_queries, dummy_metric)
```

Explanation:
- The pseudocode outlines an iterative loop where the Agentic RAG system is evaluated over multiple iterations.
- After each iteration, the average evaluation score is computed, and the system's configuration is updated if it outperforms the previous best.
- This process helps in fine-tuning hyperparameters and continuously improving system performance.

Summary

In Chapter 13, we covered the experimental design and benchmarking process for Agentic RAG systems:

- Designing Experiments: We outlined how to set up experiments using controlled datasets, baseline models, and consistent evaluation protocols.
- Evaluation Metrics: We reviewed key metrics (BLEU, ROUGE, Perplexity, BERTScore, Human Evaluation) and performance indicators such as latency and resource utilization.
- Benchmarking: We discussed how to compare Agentic RAG systems against traditional generative models and advanced hybrid approaches using controlled experiments and statistical analysis.
- Iterative Analysis and Refinement: We presented strategies for continuously improving the system through iterative experiments, hyperparameter tuning, error analysis, and A/B testing.

By following these guidelines, you can rigorously assess the performance of your Agentic RAG system, identify areas for improvement, and ensure that your system meets both quality and efficiency requirements in real-world applications.

Chapter 14: Ethical, Legal, and Societal Considerations

As AI systems become increasingly autonomous and capable of integrating vast amounts of external data with generative capabilities, it is essential to address the ethical, legal, and societal implications of their deployment. This chapter examines these issues in depth and provides best practices for developing and operating autonomous AI systems in a responsible manner.

14.1 Ethical Implications of Autonomous AI Systems

Overview

Autonomous AI systems are designed to make decisions without direct human oversight. While these systems offer efficiency, scalability, and advanced capabilities, they also raise significant ethical questions, including:

- **Accountability:**
  Determining who is responsible when an autonomous system makes a harmful or erroneous decision.
- **Bias and Fairness:**
  Ensuring that the system does not reinforce existing societal biases present in training data, which can lead to discriminatory outcomes.
- **Transparency and Explainability:**
  Making it clear how decisions are made by the system, which is particularly challenging when deep learning models are involved.
- **Autonomy vs. Human Oversight:**
  Balancing the benefits of autonomy with the need for human control, especially in high-stakes domains like healthcare or criminal justice.

Key Ethical Considerations

Ethical Aspect	Key Questions	Considerations
Accountability	Who is responsible for decisions that cause harm?	Developers, deployers, and the system design itself

Bias and Fairness	How can the system be designed to avoid reinforcing societal biases?	Diverse training data, bias audits, fairness metrics
Transparency	How can the decision-making process be made understandable to end users?	Explainable AI techniques, clear documentation
Human Oversight	What level of human intervention is necessary to ensure safe operation?	Human-in-the-loop (HITL) mechanisms, override controls

Best Practices for Ethical AI

- **Implement Explainability Tools:**
  Use techniques such as attention visualization or feature importance scoring to provide insights into model decisions.
- **Conduct Regular Bias Audits:**
  Analyze training data and system outputs for potential biases and adjust the data or model accordingly.
- **Maintain a Human-in-the-Loop (HITL):**
  Incorporate mechanisms that allow human oversight and intervention in critical decisions.
- **Establish Clear Accountability Policies:**
  Define roles and responsibilities across the lifecycle of the AI system, from design to deployment.

14.2 Privacy, Security, and Data Governance Challenges

Overview

Agentic AI systems often require access to sensitive data to function effectively. This section addresses the challenges related to privacy, security, and the governance of data used by these systems.

Privacy Concerns

- **Sensitive Data Handling:**
  AI systems may process personal or sensitive information (e.g., medical records, financial data).
- **Consent and Anonymization:**
  Data should be collected with informed consent and anonymized whenever possible to protect individual privacy.

Security Challenges

- **Data Breaches:**
  Systems that store or process sensitive data are potential targets for cyberattacks.
- **System Vulnerabilities:**
  AI models may be susceptible to adversarial attacks that manipulate inputs to produce harmful outputs.

Data Governance

- **Data Quality and Integrity:**
  Ensuring that data is accurate, up-to-date, and consistent is vital for reliable AI performance.
- **Regulatory Compliance:**
  Adhering to regulations such as the GDPR (General Data Protection Regulation) or CCPA (California Consumer Privacy Act) is critical.

Mitigation Strategies

Aspect	Challenges	Mitigation Strategies
Privacy	Handling sensitive personal data	Data anonymization, explicit consent, minimal data collection
Security	Preventing unauthorized access and breaches	Robust encryption, access controls, regular security audits
Data Governance	Maintaining data quality and regulatory compliance	Data validation, versioning, adherence to legal standards

Best Practices

- **Encrypt Data:**
  Use state-of-the-art encryption methods both for data in transit and at rest.
- **Implement Strict Access Controls:**
  Ensure only authorized personnel have access to sensitive data.
- **Regular Audits and Monitoring:**
  Conduct regular security audits and continuous monitoring to detect vulnerabilities.
- **Data Minimization:**
  Collect only the data that is necessary for the system to function effectively.

14.3 Navigating the Regulatory and Legal Landscape

Overview

The legal and regulatory environment for AI is evolving rapidly. Autonomous AI systems must comply with a range of laws and regulations that vary by jurisdiction and industry.

Key Regulatory Frameworks

- **General Data Protection Regulation (GDPR):**
  A comprehensive set of regulations in the EU that governs data protection and privacy.
- **California Consumer Privacy Act (CCPA):**
  A state law that enhances privacy rights and consumer protection for residents of California.
- **Sector-Specific Regulations:**
  Industries such as healthcare and finance have additional regulations (e.g., HIPAA for healthcare) that affect data handling and system operation.

Legal Considerations

- **Intellectual Property (IP):**
  Issues may arise over the ownership of AI-generated content and the use of copyrighted data during training.
- **Liability:**
  Determining who is legally liable when an autonomous AI system's decision causes harm.

- **Compliance:**
  Organizations must ensure their AI systems comply with all relevant legal frameworks and standards.

Strategies for Legal Navigation

- **Conduct Legal Audits:**
  Regularly review AI systems for compliance with current laws and regulations.
- **Collaborate with Legal Experts:**
  Engage legal counsel and regulatory specialists during the design and deployment phases.
- **Maintain Comprehensive Documentation:**
  Keep detailed records of data sources, model training processes, and decision-making criteria to support accountability and compliance.

14.4 Responsible AI: Societal Impact and Best Practices

Overview

Responsible AI involves developing and deploying autonomous systems in ways that maximize societal benefits while minimizing harms. This section focuses on practices that ensure AI systems are fair, transparent, and beneficial to society.

Societal Impact Considerations

- **Economic Impact:**
  Autonomous AI systems can disrupt labor markets and economic structures; strategies for workforce retraining and economic adaptation may be needed.
- **Social Equity:**
  AI systems must be designed to serve diverse populations and not exacerbate existing inequalities.
- **Environmental Impact:**
  The energy consumption of large-scale AI systems should be managed to reduce environmental footprints.

Best Practices for Responsible AI

Area	Best Practices	Desired Outcome

Inclusivity	Engage diverse stakeholders; perform regular bias audits	Equitable and fair outcomes across demographics
Transparency	Provide clear explanations of AI decision processes; publish interpretability reports	Build trust and enable accountability
Accountability	Define roles and responsibilities; set up ethical review boards	Clear assignment of responsibility and remediation
Sustainability	Optimize models for energy efficiency; consider environmental impacts	Reduced environmental footprint

Recommendations for Implementation

- **Inclusive Design:**
  Involve representatives from various demographic groups and stakeholders during the design process to ensure diverse perspectives are considered.
- **Ethical Oversight:**
  Establish ethical review boards that evaluate AI projects before and after deployment.
- **Public Communication:**
  Transparently communicate the capabilities, limitations, and potential societal impacts of AI systems to the public.
- **Sustainable Practices:**
  Invest in research and infrastructure that improve the energy efficiency of AI systems, such as model pruning and hardware optimization.

Summary

Chapter 14 has provided an exhaustive exploration of the ethical, legal, and societal considerations surrounding autonomous AI systems:

- **Ethical Implications:**
  We examined critical ethical issues such as accountability, bias, transparency, and the need for human oversight, and outlined best practices for mitigating these concerns.
- **Privacy, Security, and Data Governance:**
  We discussed the challenges of managing sensitive data, preventing security breaches, and ensuring data quality and regulatory compliance, along with strategies to address these challenges.
- **Regulatory and Legal Landscape:**
  We reviewed key regulatory frameworks such as GDPR and CCPA, highlighted legal issues like intellectual property and liability, and provided strategies for navigating this complex environment.
- **Responsible AI:**
  We detailed the societal impacts of AI systems and offered best practices for developing inclusive, transparent, and sustainable AI that benefits society as a whole.

By adhering to these guidelines and best practices, developers and organizations can ensure that their autonomous AI systems are not only innovative and efficient but also ethically sound, legally compliant, and socially responsible.

Chapter 15: Future Directions and Emerging Trends

As Agentic AI systems mature and integrate increasingly complex functionalities, the next phase of development is poised to benefit from rapid innovations in retrieval and generative technologies, next-generation decision-making algorithms, and interdisciplinary research. This chapter explores these emerging trends and offers a vision for the future evolution of autonomous AI systems.

15.1 Innovations in Retrieval and Generative Technologies

Overview

Recent advancements are reshaping the landscape of information retrieval and natural language generation. Innovations include:

- **Enhanced Dense Retrieval:**
  The use of state-of-the-art embedding models (e.g., Sentence-BERT, CLIP) to create high-quality, semantic representations for both text and images. Techniques such as cross-modal retrieval are emerging to bridge the gap between text and visual data.
- **Multi-Modal Retrieval:**
  Integrating data from multiple modalities (text, images, audio) to provide richer context. For example, combining textual data with visual context from diagrams or charts can enhance the relevancy of retrieved information.
- **Adaptive and Dynamic Retrieval Systems:**
  Systems that continuously update their indexes and refine their retrieval strategies based on user feedback and real-time data streams.
- **Advancements in Generative Models:**
  Improvements in transformer architectures (e.g., GPT-4, T5 variants) and techniques such as prompt engineering and in-context learning allow generative models to produce even more coherent, context-aware responses. New training paradigms—such as unsupervised domain adaptation and multi-task learning—further enhance generative capabilities.

Comparative Overview Table

Innovation	Description	Potential Impact

Enhanced Dense Retrieval	Improved embedding models for semantic search	Higher retrieval accuracy and relevance
Multi-Modal Retrieval	Combining text, images, and other modalities for richer context	Broader applicability across diverse domains
Adaptive Retrieval Systems	Dynamic updating of retrieval indexes based on feedback and data trends	More responsive and up-to-date retrieval performance
Advanced Generative Models	Next-generation transformers with better prompt engineering	More coherent, contextually accurate text generation
In-Context Learning	Models that learn dynamically from given context during inference	Reduced need for extensive fine-tuning

15.2 Next-Generation Decision-Making Algorithms

Overview

The decision-making component of Agentic AI systems is evolving beyond static rule-based or standard reinforcement learning methods. Next-generation algorithms focus on:

- **Meta Reinforcement Learning:**
  Enabling systems to learn how to learn, thereby adapting quickly to new environments and tasks.
- **Inverse Reinforcement Learning (IRL):**
  Inferring underlying reward structures from observed behaviors, which can be applied to optimize autonomous decision-making in complex environments.
- **Causal Inference and Decision Theory:**
  Integrating causal reasoning into decision-making processes to better handle uncertainty and predict the outcomes of actions.

- **Multi-Agent Coordination:**
  Developing algorithms that allow multiple autonomous agents to collaborate or compete effectively in shared environments.
- **Real-Time Adaptive Algorithms:**
  Incorporating online learning methods that update decision policies continuously based on real-time data and user feedback.

Comparative Overview Table

Approach	Description	Benefits
Meta Reinforcement Learning	Learning to adapt quickly across tasks	Increased adaptability and faster policy updates
Inverse Reinforcement Learning	Inferring reward structures from observed expert behavior	Improved understanding of complex decision dynamics
Causal Inference Techniques	Applying causal reasoning to predict action outcomes	More robust decision-making under uncertainty
Multi-Agent Coordination	Algorithms for effective collaboration among multiple agents	Enhanced performance in distributed, interactive settings
Real-Time Adaptive Learning	Online learning that adjusts policies continuously based on new data	Reduced latency and improved responsiveness

15.3 Open Research Challenges and Opportunities

Overview

Despite rapid advancements, several key challenges and research opportunities remain:

- **Interpretability and Explainability:**
  Deep learning models, especially those used in retrieval and generation, are often seen as "black boxes." Enhancing transparency is essential for building trust and ensuring accountability.
- **Scalability and Efficiency:**
  As models become larger and more complex, optimizing computational efficiency and resource utilization remains a significant challenge.
- **Robustness and Safety:**
  Ensuring that autonomous systems can handle adversarial inputs and operate safely in dynamic environments is critical, particularly in high-stakes applications like healthcare or autonomous vehicles.
- **Integration of Multi-Modal Data:**
  Effectively combining information from diverse data sources (text, image, audio, etc.) in a cohesive manner presents both technical and theoretical challenges.
- **Ethical and Societal Implications:**
  Addressing issues related to bias, privacy, and accountability will continue to be an important area of research.

Research Challenges Table

Challenge	Description	Opportunity for Innovation
Interpretability	Making AI decisions transparent and understandable	Development of explainable AI (XAI) techniques
Scalability and Efficiency	Optimizing model size and inference speed for real-world deployment	Research in model compression, quantization, and distillation
Robustness and Safety	Ensuring reliable performance under adversarial conditions	Techniques for adversarial training and robust model design
Multi-Modal Integration	Combining different types of data into a unified representation	Novel architectures and fusion methods for multi-modal data

Ethical and Societal Impact	Mitigating bias, ensuring privacy, and maintaining accountability	Fairness-aware algorithms and comprehensive data governance frameworks

15.4 Vision for the Future of Agentic AI Systems

Overview

Looking ahead, the future of Agentic AI systems is likely to be defined by greater integration, enhanced adaptability, and more responsible and transparent operation. Key elements of this vision include:

- **Holistic Integration:**
  Systems will seamlessly combine retrieval, generation, and decision-making with real-time learning and multi-modal data integration.
- **Human-AI Collaboration:**
  Rather than replacing human decision-makers, future systems will work alongside humans, providing robust support and augmenting human capabilities.
- **Ethical and Transparent AI:**
  Future AI systems will be designed with built-in ethical safeguards, transparency, and accountability, ensuring they benefit society while minimizing harm.
- **Sustainable and Efficient AI:**
  With growing concerns about energy consumption and environmental impact, future systems will prioritize sustainability through efficient algorithms and hardware optimization.
- **Adaptive and Personalized Systems:**
  AI systems will continuously learn and adapt to individual user needs and environmental changes, offering highly personalized and context-aware responses.

Visionary Table: Future of Agentic AI

Future Element	Description	Expected Impact
Holistic Integration	Seamless combination of retrieval, generation, and decision-making	More powerful, versatile, and adaptive systems

Human-AI Collaboration	Augmenting human decision-making with AI support	Enhanced productivity and decision quality
Ethical and Transparent AI	Inherent transparency and accountability in AI design	Increased trust, fairness, and societal acceptance
Sustainable AI	Focus on energy efficiency and environmental impact	Reduced resource consumption and carbon footprint
Adaptive and Personalized AI	Continuous learning tailored to individual needs	Improved user satisfaction and system effectiveness

Pseudocode Example: Dynamic Research Trend Aggregator

Below is a simplified pseudocode example that illustrates a future-oriented system for aggregating the latest research trends in autonomous AI. This pseudocode represents how such a system might continuously update its knowledge base using API calls and dynamic data integration.

python
```
Copy code
import requests
import json
from datetime import datetime

def fetch_latest_research(api_url, query):
    """
    Fetch the latest research articles based on a query from a research API
(e.g., arXiv).
    """
    response = requests.get(api_url, params={'search_query': query,
'sortBy': 'submittedDate', 'max_results': 5})
    articles = response.json()['articles']
    return articles

def update_trend_database(trend_db, new_articles):
    """
```

```
    Update the trend database with newly fetched articles.
    """
    current_time = datetime.now().isoformat()
    for article in new_articles:
      trend_db.append({
        'title': article['title'],
        'summary': article['summary'],
        'fetched_at': current_time
      })
    return trend_db


# Example usage:
api_url = "https://api.example.com/research"  # Placeholder API URL
query = "agentic retrieval augmented generation"
trend_db = []  # Initialize an empty trend database

# Fetch and update research trends
latest_articles = fetch_latest_research(api_url, query)
trend_db = update_trend_database(trend_db, latest_articles)

print("Updated Research Trends:")
print(json.dumps(trend_db, indent=2))
```

Explanation:

- **fetch_latest_research:** Simulates an API call to retrieve the latest research articles on a given topic.
- **update_trend_database:** Updates a local database (represented as a list) with the new articles and a timestamp.
- This pseudocode illustrates a future system that dynamically aggregates and updates research trends, supporting continuous learning and adaptation.

Summary

In Chapter 15, we examined the future directions and emerging trends in Agentic AI systems:

- **Innovations in Retrieval and Generative Technologies:**
  We discussed the evolution toward enhanced dense and multi-modal retrieval systems, adaptive indexes, and next-generation generative models.
- **Next-Generation Decision-Making Algorithms:**
  Emerging approaches such as meta reinforcement learning, inverse reinforcement learning, causal inference, and multi-agent coordination promise to further improve autonomous decision-making.
- **Open Research Challenges and Opportunities:**
  Challenges such as interpretability, scalability, robustness, multi-modal integration, and ethical considerations present significant opportunities for innovation.
- **Vision for the Future of Agentic AI Systems:**
  The future is envisioned as a domain of holistic integration, human-AI collaboration, ethical and transparent practices, sustainability, and highly adaptive, personalized systems.

By continuing to address these emerging trends and research challenges, the field of Agentic AI is poised to develop systems that are not only more powerful and efficient but also more responsible, transparent, and aligned with societal needs.

Chapter 16: Conclusion and Final Thoughts

In this final chapter, we consolidate the journey you have undertaken through the development, implementation, and evaluation of Agentic Retrieval-Augmented Generation (RAG) systems. We recap the key insights and contributions presented in the book, reflect on the overall experience, look ahead to future trends and challenges, and provide valuable resources for further exploration.

16.1 Recap of Key Insights and Contributions

Throughout the book, we have explored a broad spectrum of topics critical to understanding and building Agentic RAG systems. Key insights include:

- **Foundational Concepts:**
  We reviewed the evolution of AI, the principles of machine learning and deep learning, and the emergence of retrieval-augmented generation as a hybrid approach that combines external data retrieval with generative models.
- **System Architecture:**
  The book detailed modular architectures, explaining how to integrate retrieval, generation, and decision-making components. We emphasized design principles such as modularity, scalability, and robustness.
- **Practical Implementation:**
  Through step-by-step tutorials and code examples, we demonstrated how to build, deploy, and optimize each component of an Agentic RAG system. This included real-world applications in healthcare, financial services, customer interaction, and emerging domains like robotics and autonomous vehicles.
- **Evaluation and Benchmarking:**
  We outlined methodologies for experimental design, evaluation metrics (such as BLEU, ROUGE, perplexity, and human evaluation), and benchmarking techniques against traditional and cutting-edge models.
- **Ethical, Legal, and Societal Considerations:**
  Critical issues regarding accountability, bias, privacy, and data governance were addressed alongside strategies for responsible AI development.
- **Future Directions:**
  We discussed emerging trends and next-generation technologies in retrieval, generative models, and decision-making algorithms, and highlighted ongoing research challenges and opportunities.

Summary Table: Key Contributions

Area	Key Insights
Foundations	Evolution of AI, core machine learning and deep learning concepts, introduction to RAG
System Architecture	Modular design, integration of retrieval, generation, and decision modules, scalability and robustness
Practical Implementation	Detailed tutorials, code walkthroughs, deployment strategies, real-world case studies
Evaluation and Benchmarking	Experimental design, evaluation metrics (BLEU, ROUGE, perplexity, etc.), benchmarking methodologies
Ethical, Legal, and Societal Aspects	Accountability, bias, privacy, regulatory compliance, and responsible AI practices
Future Directions	Innovations in retrieval and generation, next-generation decision-making, research challenges and opportunities

16.2 Reflections on the Journey Through Agentic RAG

The journey through Agentic RAG has been both challenging and rewarding. As we have navigated through theoretical concepts, practical implementations, and real-world applications, several reflections emerge:

- **Interdisciplinary Integration:**
  Agentic RAG systems epitomize the convergence of multiple disciplines—including natural language processing, information retrieval, and decision theory. This integration not only enhances system performance but also broadens the scope of application.
- **Hands-On Learning:**
  The step-by-step tutorials and code examples have reinforced the importance of

practical experience. Building and testing components in real-world scenarios underscores the value of iterative development and continuous improvement.

- **Ethics and Responsibility:**
  The ethical, legal, and societal considerations discussed throughout the book remind us that technological advancement must be balanced with responsibility. The development of autonomous systems carries significant societal impact, requiring transparency, fairness, and accountability at every stage.
- **Continuous Evolution:**
  The field of AI is rapidly evolving. While this book provides a comprehensive foundation, it is clear that continuous learning and adaptation are essential. New challenges and opportunities will emerge, necessitating ongoing research and development.

16.3 Future Outlook and Call to Action

Future Outlook

Looking ahead, the future of Agentic AI systems is bright and full of potential:

- **Holistic Integration:**
  Future systems will achieve even greater levels of integration, combining advanced retrieval techniques, state-of-the-art generative models, and sophisticated decision-making algorithms into unified, adaptive platforms.
- **Human-AI Collaboration:**
  The trend is shifting from purely autonomous systems to collaborative models where AI augments human decision-making, resulting in improved outcomes across industries.
- **Responsible and Transparent AI:**
  As ethical and regulatory frameworks mature, the development of responsible AI will become increasingly central. Transparency, explainability, and fairness will be key drivers of public trust and societal acceptance.
- **Sustainable and Scalable Solutions:**
  Future research will focus on optimizing efficiency, reducing energy consumption, and ensuring that AI systems can scale sustainably to meet global challenges.

Call to Action

We encourage you, the reader, to:

- **Engage in Continuous Learning:**
  Stay informed about the latest advancements in AI by participating in research, attending conferences, and engaging with the community.
- **Experiment and Innovate:**
  Apply the principles and techniques from this book to your projects. Experiment with new models, architectures, and strategies to push the boundaries of what is possible.
- **Champion Responsible AI:**
  Advocate for ethical practices and transparency in AI development. Ensure that your work considers the broader societal impacts and contributes to the public good.
- **Collaborate and Share:**
  Contribute to open-source projects, collaborate with peers, and share your findings. Collective progress in AI relies on the exchange of ideas and collaborative problem-solving.

16.4 Resources for Continued Learning and Research

To further your knowledge and stay updated on developments in Agentic RAG and related fields, consider the following resources:

Books and Publications

- **"Deep Learning" by Ian Goodfellow, Yoshua Bengio, and Aaron Courville:**
  A comprehensive resource on deep learning fundamentals.
- **"Natural Language Processing with Transformers" by Lewis Tunstall, Leandro von Werra, and Thomas Wolf:**
  A practical guide to building NLP applications using transformer models.
- **Recent Research Papers:**
  Stay current with publications on arXiv, IEEE Xplore, and ACM Digital Library in the areas of retrieval, generation, and autonomous decision-making.

Online Courses and Tutorials

- **Coursera, edX, and Udacity:**
  Offer courses on machine learning, deep learning, and AI ethics.
- **Hugging Face Courses:**
  Free courses and tutorials on transformer models and NLP applications.

- **Fast.ai:**
  Practical deep learning courses with a focus on implementation.

Communities and Conferences

- **AI Conferences:**
  Attend events such as NeurIPS, ICML, ACL, and CVPR to network and learn about the latest research.
- **Online Communities:**
  Engage with communities on GitHub, Stack Overflow, Reddit (e.g., r/MachineLearning), and specialized forums.
- **Workshops and Meetups:**
  Participate in local AI meetups and workshops to share knowledge and gain insights from practitioners.

Websites and Blogs

- **Hugging Face Blog:**
  Regular updates on the latest advancements in transformer models and NLP.
- **Towards Data Science:**
  Articles and tutorials on various aspects of AI and machine learning.
- **AI Alignment Forum:**
  Discussions on the ethical and technical challenges of aligning AI with human values.

Example: Resource List Table

Resource Type	Name/Link	Description
Book	*Deep Learning* by Goodfellow et al.	Comprehensive guide to deep learning fundamentals.
Online Course	Hugging Face Course	Free tutorials on transformers and NLP applications.
Conference	NeurIPS, ICML, ACL	Premier conferences for AI and machine learning research.

Research Repository	arXiv.org	Preprint server for the latest research papers.
Community Forum	r/MachineLearning on Reddit	Community discussions and insights on machine learning topics.

Summary

In this final chapter, we have:

- **Recapped Key Insights and Contributions:**
  Summarizing the foundational theories, system architectures, implementation strategies, evaluation techniques, and ethical considerations discussed throughout the book.
- **Reflected on the Journey:**
  Emphasizing the interdisciplinary nature of Agentic RAG, the value of hands-on learning, and the importance of ethical and responsible AI development.
- **Outlined a Future Outlook and Call to Action:**
  Highlighting emerging trends, the promise of human-AI collaboration, and encouraging continued learning and innovation.
- **Provided Resources for Continued Learning:**
  Offering a curated list of books, courses, conferences, and communities to support your ongoing journey in AI research and development.

Appendices

The appendices provide supplementary materials to support the main content of this book. They include detailed code examples and tutorials to reinforce practical understanding, a glossary to clarify technical terms, a curated list of research papers and further readings for deeper exploration, and biographical information along with acknowledgements for those who contributed to this work.

A.1 Code Examples and Detailed Tutorials

This section contains a collection of code examples and step-by-step tutorials designed to help you implement the concepts discussed in the book. Each example is accompanied by clear explanations and comments to ensure that the code is both understandable and practical.

Example 1: Basic Retrieval Module

Below is a Python code example that demonstrates how to implement a simple retrieval module using keyword matching.

python
Copy code
```python
# retrieval_module.py

class RetrievalModule:
    def __init__(self, corpus):
        """
        Initialize the Retrieval Module with a corpus.
        :param corpus: List of documents (strings)
        """
        self.corpus = corpus

    def retrieve(self, query):
        """
        Retrieve documents that contain any of the words in the query.
        :param query: Input query string
        :return: List of matching documents
        """
        query_words = query.lower().split()
```

```python
        matching_docs = []
        for doc in self.corpus:
            # Check if any query word is present in the document
            if any(word in doc.lower() for word in query_words):
                matching_docs.append(doc)
        return matching_docs

# Example usage:
if __name__ == "__main__":
    corpus = [
        "Agentic RAG systems integrate retrieval and generation.",
        "Retrieval modules provide essential context for decision-making.",
        "Generative models create coherent responses based on context."
    ]
    retrieval = RetrievalModule(corpus)
    query = "retrieval decision"
    results = retrieval.retrieve(query)
    print("Retrieved Documents:")
    for doc in results:
        print("-", doc)
```

Explanation:

- The RetrievalModule class initializes with a corpus (a list of documents).
- The retrieve method splits the input query into words, converts text to lowercase for case-insensitive matching, and returns documents containing any of the query words.

Example 2: Simple Decision Engine

Below is a code example for a rule-based decision engine that decides whether to generate a detailed response based on the number of retrieved documents.

python
Copy code
```python
# decision_engine.py

class DecisionEngine:
    def __init__(self, threshold=3):
        """
        Initialize the Decision Engine with a decision threshold.
```

```python
        :param threshold: Minimum number of documents required to
generate a detailed response.
        """
        self.threshold = threshold

    def decide(self, retrieved_docs):
        """
        Decide on an action based on the number of retrieved documents.
        :param retrieved_docs: List of documents retrieved from the retrieval
module.
        :return: Decision string.
        """
        if len(retrieved_docs) >= self.threshold:
            return "generate_detailed_response"
        else:
            return "request_more_information"

# Example usage:
if __name__ == "__main__":
    docs = ["doc1", "doc2"]
    engine = DecisionEngine(threshold=3)
    decision = engine.decide(docs)
    print("Decision:", decision)
```

Explanation:

- The DecisionEngine class uses a threshold to determine whether enough documents have been retrieved.
- The decide method returns "generate_detailed_response" if the number of documents meets or exceeds the threshold; otherwise, it returns "request_more_information".

Additional Tutorials

In this appendix, you will also find detailed tutorials for:

- **Integrating Retrieval, Generation, and Decision Modules:** Step-by-step guides that show how to create an end-to-end pipeline.
- **Fine-Tuning Generative Models:** Walkthroughs on using libraries such as Hugging Face Transformers for model fine-tuning.

- **Performance Optimization Techniques:** Tutorials on caching, parallel processing, and deploying models in cloud environments using Docker and Kubernetes.

Each tutorial includes complete code examples, screenshots where applicable, and clear commentary to facilitate self-paced learning.

A.2 Glossary of Technical Terms and Acronyms

This glossary provides definitions for key terms and acronyms used throughout the book. It is intended to serve as a quick reference to help you understand technical jargon and concepts.

Term/Acronym	Definition
Agentic AI	AI systems capable of autonomous decision-making and adapting to new information in real time.
RAG (Retrieval- Augmented Generation)	A hybrid approach that combines external data retrieval with generative models to enhance response quality.
Transformer	A type of neural network architecture that uses self-attention mechanisms to process sequential data efficiently.
BERT	Bidirectional Encoder Representations from Transformers, designed for natural language understanding tasks.
GPT	Generative Pre-trained Transformer, a family of models used primarily for text generation.
T5	Text-to-Text Transfer Transformer, a model that frames all NLP tasks as text-to-text problems.

FAISS	Facebook AI Similarity Search, a library for efficient similarity search and clustering of dense vectors.
API	Application Programming Interface, a set of routines and protocols for building software applications.
CI/CD	Continuous Integration/Continuous Deployment, practices that allow for frequent and reliable software updates.
HITL	Human-in-the-Loop, a system design paradigm where human judgment is integrated into the decision-making process.
BLEU	Bilingual Evaluation Understudy, an automated metric for evaluating the quality of text generated by AI models.
ROUGE	Recall-Oriented Understudy for Gisting Evaluation, a set of metrics for evaluating summarization quality.
Perplexity	A measurement of how well a probability model predicts a sample, with lower values indicating better performance.
GDPR	General Data Protection Regulation, an EU regulation on data protection and privacy.
CCPA	California Consumer Privacy Act, a state law enhancing privacy rights for California residents.

A.3 Comprehensive List of Research Papers and Further Reading

For readers interested in exploring the topics covered in this book further, the following list of research papers and publications provides a comprehensive resource.

Selected Research Papers

Title	Authors	Publication/ Year	Link/Reference
"Attention Is All You Need"	Vaswani et al.	2017	arXiv:1706.03762
"BERT: Pre-training of Deep Bidirectional Transformers"	Devlin et al.	2018	arXiv:1810.04805
"Language Models are Few-Shot Learners"	Brown et al.	2020	arXiv:2005.14165
"Retrieval-Augmented Generation for Knowledge-Intensive NLP Tasks"	Lewis et al.	2020	arXiv:2005.11401
"Dense Passage Retrieval for Open-Domain Question Answering"	Karpukhin et al.	2020	arXiv:2004.04906

Further Reading

- **Books:**
    - *Deep Learning* by Ian Goodfellow, Yoshua Bengio, and Aaron Courville.
    - *Natural Language Processing with Transformers* by Lewis Tunstall, Leandro von Werra, and Thomas Wolf.
- **Online Courses:**
    - Hugging Face Courses for transformers and NLP.
    - Coursera and edX courses on deep learning and machine learning fundamentals.
- **Websites and Blogs:**
    - Hugging Face Blog: https://huggingface.co/blog
    - Towards Data Science: https://towardsdatascience.com

Preface
- Acknowledgements
- About the Author(s)
- How to Use This Book
- Overview of the Agentic RAG Landscape

Chapter 1: Introduction
1.1. The Evolution of AI and the Rise of Autonomy
  - Historical Context and Motivations
1.2. Defining Retrieval-Augmented Generation (RAG)
  - From Pure Generation to Hybrid Models
1.3. What Makes a System "Agentic"?
  - Integrating Autonomous Decision-Making
1.4. Scope, Audience, and Objectives of the Book
1.5. Structure and Roadmap

Chapter 2: Theoretical Foundations in AI and Autonomous Systems
2.1. Core Concepts in Machine Learning and Deep Learning
2.2. An Introduction to Decision Theory and Reinforcement Learning
2.3. Neural Architectures: From RNNs to Transformers
2.4. Overview of Retrieval Techniques and Algorithms

Chapter 3: Fundamentals of Retrieval-Augmented Generation (RAG)
3.1. The RAG Paradigm: Principles and Evolution
3.2. Key Components: Retrieval Module vs. Generative Module
3.3. Comparative Analysis with Traditional AI Models
3.4. Recent Advances and State-of-the-Art Innovations

Chapter 4: Autonomous Decision-Making in AI
4.1. Defining Autonomy: Concepts and Terminology
4.2. Decision-Making Frameworks: Rule-Based, Learning-Based, and Hybrid
4.3. Reinforcement Learning and Policy Optimization
4.4. Multi-Agent Systems and Distributed Decision Making

Chapter 5: Architecting Agentic RAG Systems
5.1. Design Principles and Modular Architectures